STANDING ON THE PROMISES

OR

SITTING ON THE PREMISES?

JAMES W. MOORE

Standing on the PROMISES

— OR —

Sitting on the PREMISES?

DIMENSIONS
FOR LIVING

NASHVILLE

STANDING ON THE PROMISES OR SITTING ON THE PREMISES?

Library of Congress Cataloging-in-Publication Data

Moore, James W. (James Wendell), 1938–
  Standing on the promises or sitting on the premises? / James W. Moore.—[Rev. ed.].
      p. cm.
  "Study guide and new chapters 11 and 14"—T.p. verso.
  ISBN 978-0-687-64254-0 (pbk.: alk. paper)
  1. Christian life. 2. God (Christianity)—Promises. I. Title.
  BV4501.3.M66455 2007
  248.4—dc22

                                                                    2007009350

In honor of the members and staff of St. Luke's United Methodist Church in Houston, Texas

Contents

Introduction

Are You Standing on the Promises or Sitting on the Premises?

Let me begin with a question: "Are you standing on the promises, or just sitting on the premises?" That is, do you claim and embrace and celebrate the great promises of God, underscored again and again in the Bible? Or do you just sit listlessly on the remote edges of the church and respond halfheartedly to its message? Do God's promises inspire you, invigorate you, and strengthen you for the living of these days? Or do you forget those promises or ignore them, and consequently trudge sluggishly through life, with no zest, no fire, no heart, no excitement, no mission, and no purpose?

One of the problems is that some people do indeed seem to forget God's awesome promises in the Bible. Forgetting—not remembering—can be a real setup for embarrassing and frustrating experiences. And our "forgetfulness" becomes worse as we get older.

Let me tell you what I mean. Have you heard about the couple who discovered a new restaurant? They loved it. It was a great experience. The very next night, some friends dropped by, and as the wife went into the kitchen to prepare the coffee, the husband proceeded to tell the friends about this new restaurant they had found: "The food was sumptuous, the service outstanding, the decor was perfect, and the price was right."

The friends said, "That sounds wonderful. What is the name of the restaurant?"

"Oh my goodness," said the man. "I was afraid you were going to ask me that. I can't remember. I'm getting so forgetful, it's ridiculous. I can't remember anything anymore! Wait a minute," he went on, "I have an idea. What is that beautiful flower that has a long stem and a beautiful blossom, and thorns?"

They suggested, "A rose?"

"That's right," he answered, and, turning toward the kitchen, he shouted, "Hey Rose! Please come here and tell them the name of that restaurant we went to last night!" Now, that's what you call forgetful! And, unfortunately, too many of us have that problem.

Jesus knew full well how forgetful we can be, so again and again he repeated for us one of the greatest promises in the Bible: The gift of the Holy Spirit—the promise of the Holy Spirit!

"Remember now," he said to his disciples (and to us), "I will not leave you alone! I will not desert you or forsake you. I will not leave you desolate. I will be with you always, even to the end of the world. If you will put your faith in me and trust in me, come what may, I will be there for you. You will be clothed with power from on high. The Holy Spirit will come to you. The Holy Spirit will be your strength. The Holy Spirit will do great things for you and through you. The Holy Spirit will see you through" (John 14:15-17 adapted).

If that great promise doesn't excite you or thrill you or encourage you, then you need to check your spiritual pulse or put a spiritual stethoscope to your heart. That's what that powerful passage in John 14 is all about. Jesus is in the upper room with his disciples. The cross looms near. Why, the very next day is Good Friday! Jesus is giving them their final instructions. Scholars refer to this section in John as "The Farewell Discourses" of Jesus. Here in chapters 13, 14, and 15 we see Jesus giving his disciples their marching orders—a series of promises and a series of last-minute reminders.

The gist of these three chapters is capsuled in two verses: "If you love me, you will keep my commandments. And I will ask the Father, and he will give you another Advocate, to be with you forever. This is the Spirit of truth" (John 14:15-17*a*). What a great promise this is—the Holy Spirit of God to be ever present with us, giving us strength, support, inspiration, and power!

That's the promise I want us to remember, to embrace, to celebrate, and to stand on today—and all the days ahead. God promises to always be with us. That is the good news of our Christian faith. Let me bring this closer to home with three thoughts.

First, God Promises to Be with Us Through the Holy Spirit to Give Us Comfort

Now, the word *comfort* literally means "with strength." Those who are comforted are those who are given strength.

Some years ago, a young friend of mine was stricken with leukemia. A bright student, an outstanding musician, a warm and radiant personality, a devoted Christian, a loyal friend—she was all of that and much, much more.

The leukemia was diagnosed two days after Courtney's fifteenth birthday. During the next two years, she and her family made twenty-seven trips to Saint Jude Children's Hospital in Memphis. She was seventeen when she died. When word came that Courtney had died, I went over to see her family. I didn't know what to say. What do you say to parents who have just lost a child? I rang the doorbell.

Courtney's mom answered the door, and before I could say a word, she greeted me: "Oh Jim, I'm so glad you've come. Come on into the kitchen and let's get a cup of coffee and talk about Courtney. She was so wonderful and we have so many precious memories." We sat and sipped our coffee and reminisced about Courtney. We poured our hearts out right there at the kitchen table. We cried as we remembered the painful moments. We laughed as we remembered her incredible sense of humor through it all—some of the funny things she had said and done. And we prayed when we recalled her amazing faith, her tender love, and her brave spirit!

Finally, when I stood to leave, Courtney's mom took my hand, looked me straight in the eye, and said, "Now, Jim, don't you worry about us. We're going to be all right. This is the toughest thing we have ever been through—no question about that—but God is with us as never before, and he will hold us up, he will see us through. He has given us strength every day throughout this ordeal, and he will give us the strength we need now to go on with life as a tribute to Courtney."

I was so touched by her spiritual poise and confidence, and I realized something: I had gone there to minister to her, and she had ministered to me! As I drove away, her words kept reverberating in my head: "God is with us as never before." Why is that? I thought to myself. Why do we feel the presence of God "as never before" when we are hurting? For people of faith, why does God feel closer when we are in pain? Two reasons came to mind:

1. When we are in trouble, we are more open to God, we tend to tune in more to God, we tend to realize more how very much we need him.

2. Jesus taught us that God is like a loving parent, and loving parents want to be with their children most of all when the children are hurting. They want to be with them and bring help and strength and comfort.

Isn't this a great promise to stand on? Again and again and again in the Scriptures, God promises to be with us through the Holy Spirit, to give us comfort.

Second, God Promises to Be with Us Through the Holy Spirit to Give Us Courage

In a philosophy class at Rice University, the professor told the students to bring blue books for a test next time. On test day, the professor said to the class, "Your test today is to write an essay on the topic, 'What is Courage?'" The students began to write furiously. All, that is, except one young man. He sat there quietly for five minutes, thinking deeply. He then picked up his pen and wrote the title, "What Is Courage?" Then he wrote down two more words—just two words—and turned in his test, and walked out of the classroom.

Most students took the full hour and filled all the pages of their blue books on the subject of courage. That evening the professor telephoned the young man who had turned in the two-word essay and informed him that he had given him an A+ on the test. He added that he would like to get to know the student better.

I suspect that you are already trying to figure out what those two words were, as I was when I first heard this story. The two words the student wrote in answer to the question, "What is Courage?" were this: THIS IS.

(Thanks to Busher Fanning, Trinity Baptist Church, San Antonio, Texas, for this story.)

You see what he did? He didn't just define courage. He demonstrated it. He acted it out. That was a "gutsy" and creative thing to do in the academic arena. That's one kind of courage, but there is another kind that is even better, and that is the courage that comes from knowing that God is with you.

Some years ago, when an American was visiting the city of Damascus, he went to the famous marketplace on the street called Straight. The marketplace was busy, crowded, teeming with merchants and shoppers and tourists. Into that bustling place came a man riding slowly through the crowd on a bicycle, precariously balancing a basket of oranges on the handle bars. He was bumped accidentally by a porter who was so bent over, carrying a heavy burden, that he had not seen him. The burden dropped, the oranges were scattered, and a bitter altercation broke out between the cyclist and the porter.

Angry words, threats, hostilities were shouted. A crowd gathered to watch what was certain to become a bloody fight. The enraged cyclist moved toward the porter with a clenched fist. But just then, a tattered little man stepped out of the crowd and positioned himself between the adversaries. Then the little man did an amazing thing. He reached out, tenderly took the cyclist's clenched fist in his hands, and gently kissed it! He kissed the fist! A murmur of approval swept over the crowd. They laughed, then they applauded. The antagonists relaxed and hugged each other. And all the people began happily picking up the oranges.

When the little man began to drift away, the American followed him and spoke to him: "What a brave and beautiful thing you did! That was wonderful, but why did you do it? Why did you risk it?"

The little man smiled and answered, "Because I am a Christian! The Spirit of Christ was in me, and he gave me the courage to be a peacemaker. He gave me the courage to do the right thing."

Isn't that a great promise to stand on? Again and again in the Bible, God promises to be with us through the Holy Spirit, to give us comfort and to give us courage.

Third, God Promises to Give Us a Commission—a Special Job to Do

Remember Margaret Deeney's poem, "Proud Words":

'Tis sweet to hear "I love you"
Beneath a giggling moon;

'Tis fun to hear "You dance well"
To a lilting, swinging tune;
'Tis great to be proposed to
And whisper low, "I do";
But the greatest words in all the world,
"I've got a job for you!"

This is one of God's greatest promises and greatest gifts to us. God says:

• I've got a job for you.
• You are valuable to me.
• There is something special I want you to do.
• Take up this torch, take up this ministry, and I will help you.

Late one night in Paris, Albert Schweitzer came home, exhausted and weary, from the university where he was a professor. Hurriedly, he looked through his mail so that he could get to bed. But a magazine with a green cover caught his eye. Feeling drawn to it, he flipped through the pages and suddenly was captivated by an article titled, "The Needs of the Congo Mission," written by Alfred Boegner.

"As I sit here in Africa (Boegner wrote), it is my prayer that the eyes of someone on whom the eye of God has already fallen will read and be awakened to the call and say, 'Here am I.'"

Moved by Boegner's earnest appeal for someone to help him in the Congo, Schweitzer bowed his head and prayed, "My search has ended, I am coming."

Thus awakened, Schweitzer studied medicine at the University of Strasbourg, and in 1913, sailed to French Equatorial Africa, where his first jungle hospital was a chicken coop in Lambaréné.

When he made that decision to answer God's call to become a medical missionary, Albert Schweitzer was...

...a noted author,

...a highly respected musician,

...an established theologian,

...the pastor of a church,

...principal of Saint Thomas Theological College at the University of Strasbourg, and

...the greatest living organ interpreter of the works of Bach.

(Pulpit Resource, Oct./Nov./Dec. 1989)

But Schweitzer had felt God calling him to a special job, so he turned his back on the prestige, power, and promise that were his and gave his life to God's work in Africa. The rest is amazing history—all because he heard the call of God and said, "Here am I, Lord, send me." Some could not understand how Albert Schweitzer could leave behind "the good life" in Europe, but somewhere in heaven, God was smiling.

What great promises! On page after page of the Scriptures, God promises to be with us through the Holy Spirit—to give us comfort, courage, and a commission. And as we study the Bible closely, we discover that many other great promises are recorded in the Scriptures—generous and gracious promises from God, promises that we can claim and rely on and trust. But still, the question is: Are we standing on those promises, or are we just sitting on the premises?

1

The Promise of God's Love

The Greatest Gift

JOHN 3:16

For God so loved the world that he gave his only
Son, so that everyone who believes in him may not
perish but may have eternal life.

Bennett Cerf was a respected publisher and author for
Random House a few years ago. Because of his keen
intellect and warm sense of humor, he was often featured
as a panelist on numerous television and radio programs.
Some of you will remember seeing him on those early
popular TV shows like "What's My Line?" and "I've Got
a Secret."

One evening he appeared on an NBC radio program
called "Conversation." The panelists on this particular
show were asked to spend the entire thirty-minute program that night discussing just one question: "What Are
You Most Afraid Of?" The panelists went at it, dialogu-
ing and debating that topic for more than twenty minutes. They talked about a wide range of fears, but finally
they decided on the one thing they were most afraid of:
"annihilation by the nuclear bomb."

After the panelists had reached that consensus, the
moderator, Clifton Fadiman, noticed that Bennett Cerf
had been unusually quiet throughout the vigorous discussion. In fact, he hadn't said a word. When prodded,

Cerf replied in a humble voice that he had hesitated to answer the question truthfully because he was afraid that his concern would seem so trivial beside the vast issues that others had introduced.

But he went on to say that since the point of the program was to share what you really thought, he might as well admit that what he feared most was "not being loved." Bennett Cerf was a smart and honest man. He knew about the importance of love. And he was right on target that night. For there is nothing more destructive to the human heart than to live without love. As Dr. Smiley Blanton once put it: "We love or we perish!"

Now, if I were to ask you to write down what you consider the single greatest verse of Scripture in the whole Bible, what would you put down? Of course, there would be a variety of answers given, I'm sure, but in all likelihood, the verse most written down would be John 3:16: "For God so loved the world that he gave his only Son, so that everyone who believes in him may not perish but may have eternal life."

With good reason, many people would select John 3:16. This single verse is a magnificent summary of the gospel, the message of the Scriptures in capsule form. It is the story of God's seeking, redeeming, reconciling love, all in one sentence. It has been called "everybody's text." Here, for every simple heart, is the essence of the Christian faith and "good news," and God's greatest promise.

This verse reminds us that we are indeed loved and that God himself is the one who loves us; that God seeks us out, that God values us, that God graciously reaches out to save us, and that when we (in faith) accept God's love, we can have life eternal. We see this verse acted out dramatically during Holy Week.

On Palm Sunday, Jesus rides triumphantly into the Holy City. He is received as a king, with palm branches strewn before him and loud Hosannas ringing in the air.

But he comes to establish a surprising kingdom, one different from anything our world has ever seen—one built not on power and violence and might, but rather a kingdom built on faith and hope and love. Through the days of Holy Week, he teaches the people, heals the sick, helps the needy, cleanses the Temple, and withstands, with amazing spiritual dexterity and wisdom, the tricky, loaded questions fired at him by the chief priests and elders who are trying to entrap him.

He tenderly takes the disciples through the last supper, and then he goes into the Garden of Gethsemane to pray. There he is betrayed by one of his closest friends, arrested on trumped-up charges, rushed through a hurried fixed trial that takes place illegally in the middle of the night, and is sentenced to death by crucifixion by a waffling Pontius Pilate.

And then on Good Friday (which, by the way, originally was called God's Friday), in the greatest act of sacrificial love this world has ever known, he goes to the cross and dies there for you and me. "For God so loved the world that he gave his only Son, so that everyone who believes in him may not perish but may have eternal life."

No question about it, John 3:16 is one of the greatest statements ever spoken, because it describes, defines, and outlines the fullness of God's redeeming love. The verse falls neatly into three parts, showing us the width of God's love, the depth of God's love, and the power of God's love.

First, We See the Width of God's Love

Look at the very first phrase: "For God so loved the world"—not just one nation, not just one culture, not just one denomination, not just the attractive people, not just one little corner of creation, but the whole world! As the famous spiritual puts it: "He's Got the Whole World in His Hands." In a word, the reach of God's love is as wide as the universe.

One sad thing that happens to us human beings is that we often forget the bigness of God's love, and consequently, we become small and selective in our loving, limiting our love to only a favored few. Not so with God. God's love leaps over every barrier to embrace every person. And as human beings, we become impatient with people who don't act as we want them to act or do what we want them to do.

The great Protestant Reformer Martin Luther once became so aggravated with those around him that he cried out, "If I were God and these vile people were as disobedient as they now be, I would knock the world to pieces!" And Luther might have done that, but not so with God. The Bible underscores again and again the amazing grace of God, and this verse (as no other) shows the enormous sweep of God's gracious forgiving, seeking, reconciling love for the whole world. We may reject God's love. We may run away from God's love. We may ignore God's love. And our own hardness of heart may keep us out of God's kingdom, may keep us from accepting God's love in faith. But one thing we can know, one thing we can count on: God loves us, and God wants to bring us into the circle of his love.

It's important to remember now that although God's love is worldwide, it is yet very personal. Even though God's love is vast enough to reach around the globe, still it is closer to each and every one of us than our breathing.

Remember the "Peanuts" comic strip in which Lucy announces that she wants to be a doctor when she grows up. Younger brother, Linus, is very upset by the prospect, and he says, "Lucy, it won't work. You can never be a doctor!"

"And just why not?" Lucy retorts.

"Because," replies Linus, "you don't love humankind. You can't be a doctor because you don't love humankind!"

"But I do," says Lucy, "I do! I love humankind; it's *people* I can't stand!"

Not so with God. He loves the whole world, and he loves all the people in it. Do you see what this means? It means that you are the beloved child of God, that I am the beloved child of God, and that every single person we meet in this world is the beloved child of God. The message is obvious: Accept God's love for you and love God back, and pass God's love on to others in this world. Here we see the width of God's love—"For God so loved the world."

Second, We See the Depth of God's Love

God's love is wide and it is deep. Here's how John's Gospel records it: "For God so loved the world that he gave his only Son." Talk about depth of love. He gave his only son!

You are aware of the fact that the New Testament was written originally in the Greek language and that the common Greek had several different words for love. The three most familiar of these are:

- EROS—which gives us our word *erotic*;
- PHILIA—which gives us our word *philanthropist*; and
- AGAPE—the word used throughout the New Testament to describe God's love.

In capsule form, eros refers to sensual love; philia refers to social love; agape refers to sacrificial love. God's sacrificial love is what we see in Jesus Christ. God so loves the world that he gives his only son to save it.

In *Becoming a Whole Person in a Broken World*, Ron Lee Davis tells about a young woman named Marie who was admitted to a mental hospital in Europe. She was in a terrible emotional state. She had been reared by violent, abusive parents. At age twelve, she saw her mother and father in a horrible drunken argument one night. They were fighting and struggling over a gun. Suddenly, the pistol fired, and before young Marie's eyes, her father fell dead!

Little Marie's mind snapped. She was filled with pain, frustration, and hatred. She retreated into a fantasy world, but it too was violent. Marie would scream, scratch, hit, and curse at anyone who came near her. She was placed alone in a padded cell. The attending physician tried several approaches, to no avail. She seemed only to become worse. Finally, the doctor decided to try a then common therapy called catharsis—the venting of rage upon someone else.

A nurse named Hulda volunteered to be the victim. Every day, Hulda would enter Marie's padded cell. For a full hour, Marie would curse, kick, scream, hit, and scratch Hulda. Then exhausted, Marie would crouch in a corner like a frightened animal, and the nurse Hulda (battered, bruised, and sometimes bleeding) would go to Marie and hold the child tenderly in her arms, rock her gently, and say over and over, "Marie, I love you. Marie, I love you."

Little by little, this message of love got through. Little by little, Marie was able to respond with tears and affection. And in time, Marie was well. She became a whole person. She was healed by sacrificial love. On a deeper level, that's the kind of deep love God gives to us in Jesus Christ. As the Scriptures put it, "By his stripes we are healed."

Here in John 3:16, we see the width of God's love (he loved the whole world), and we see the depth of God's sacrificial love (he gave his only son).

Finally, We See the Power of God's Love

God's love is a love so powerful that it can redeem and reconcile and save. Listen to it again: "For God so loved the world that he gave his only Son, so that everyone who believes in him may not perish but may have eternal life."

Author Walter Wangerin tells a wonderful story about an experience he had some years ago with his son. When Matthew was seven years old and in the second grade, he became fascinated with comic books. So much so, that one day he stole some from the library. When Walter found the comic books in Matthew's room, he confronted him, corrected him, disciplined him, and took him back to the library to return the books. Matthew received a stern lecture regarding stealing from the librarian and also from his dad.

The following summer, however, it happened again. Matthew stole some comic books from a resort gift shop. Again Walter corrected him and told him how wrong it was to steal. A year later, Matthew once again stole comic books from a drug store. Walter decided he had to do something to get his attention and to underscore the seriousness of stealing.

So he took Matthew into his study and said, "Matthew, I have never spanked you before, and I don't want to now, but somehow I've got to get through to you and help you see how wrong it is to steal." So Walter bent Matthew over and spanked him five times with his bare hand. Matthew's eyes moistened with tears, and he sat there looking at the floor.

His father said, "Matthew, I'm going to leave you alone for a little while. You sit here, and I'll be back in a few minutes."

Walter stepped out of the study and he just couldn't help himself; he broke down and cried like a baby. The father cried and cried. Then he washed his face and went back into the study to talk to his little son. From that moment, Matthew never stole again. In fact, to the contrary, he became a generous, giving person.

Years later, as Matthew and his mother were driving

home from a shopping center, they began to talk about some memories of his childhood. They remembered the incident with the comic books.

Matthew said, "Mom, after that, I never stole anything again from anybody, and I never will."

His mother asked, "Was it because your dad spanked you that day?"

"Oh no," Matthew explained, "It was because I heard him crying!" It wasn't the spanking that turned Matthew's life around; it was the power of his father's love.

God's love is so powerful that it can sustain us all through this life, and it can take us all the way to heaven. But please don't miss this. The text says, "Everyone who believes in him may not perish." That means we must accept God's love in faith. The Greek word for *believe* is "pisteo" which literally means *faithful, believing, obedience.* It means believing in God and his love so much that we stake our lives on God and commit our lives, heart and soul, to God.

Do you believe like that? Have you accepted the power of God's redeeming love into your life? If not, do it today! Don't waste another moment. Let God into your heart. Don't miss out on the greatest promise and the greatest gift this world has ever known.

2

The Promise of God's Presence with Us

Where the Risen Christ Meets Us

JOHN 21:15-19

When they had finished breakfast, Jesus said to Simon Peter, "Simon son of John, do you love me more than these?" He said to him, "Yes, Lord; you know that I love you." Jesus said to him, "Feed my lambs." A second time he said to him, "Simon son of John, do you love me?" He said to him, "Yes, Lord; you know that I love you." Jesus said to him, "Tend my sheep." He said to him the third time, "Simon son of John, do you love me?" Peter felt hurt because he said to him the third time, "Do you love me?" And he said to him, "Lord, you know everything; you know that I love you." Jesus said to him, "Feed my sheep. Very truly, I tell you, when you were younger, you used to fasten your own belt and to go wherever you wished. But when you grow old, you will stretch out your hands, and someone else will fasten a belt around you and take you where you do not wish to go." (He said this to indicate the kind of death by which he would glorify God.) After this he said to him, "Follow me."

On display in the magnificent Louvre Museum in Paris, France, is that dramatic painting of Goethe's *Faust*. Faust is seated at a table engaged in a competitive game of chess. And at first glance, it looks as if Faust is losing. His opponent is Mephistopheles, the devil of medieval legend. The devil sits there grinning smugly. He thinks he has the victory in hand. He is pointing at the chessboard gloating with an evil leer.

As you look at the painting, you can almost hear the devil shouting, "Checkmate! Game's over! I win!" However, one with a keen eye who knows the game of chess can see that the match is not over at all. As a matter of fact, just a few years ago, an internationally famous chess player was admiring the painting, when suddenly he lunged forward and exclaimed, "Wait a minute! Look! Faust has another move, and that move will give him the victory!"

That painting is something of a parable for us Christians, because there we see symbolized the good news of our faith.

Think of it. When we look at the cross on Good Friday, it looks (at first glance) as if evil has won. It looks like the defeat of righteousness. It looks as if goodness is dead and buried forever. It looks as if Christ has been silenced and conquered.

But then, on Easter morning, God's move is revealed, the greatest checkmate move of all time. Christ comes out of the grave and into our lives with power and victory.

Sometimes it does feel that evil is winning, but then along comes Easter to remind us that there is no grave deep enough, no seal imposing enough, no stone heavy enough, no wickedness strong enough to keep Christ in the grave. He will win. God and goodness will win. God and truth will win. God and love will win. And with amazing grace, God wants to share that victory with you and me. What a promise to stand on!

That is precisely what this touching passage in John 21

is about. Christ is resurrected and comes looking for Simon Peter. At crunch time, Simon Peter had failed; he had denied his Lord. Not once, not twice, but three times, he had denied his Lord! He needs forgiveness, reassurance. He needs new life. So the Risen Christ comes to meet him and give him what he needs. That's the good news of the Christian faith for us. Christ not only conquers evil and death, but he also resurrects us. That's what John 21 teaches us.

Remember the story with me. Some months earlier, Simon had left his fishing nets at the seashore to become a follower of Jesus. Jesus liked Simon. He included him in his closest circle of friends. He changed Simon's name to Peter (Petros, the Rock) because Jesus felt that he was strong, stable, and solid, like a rock.

But suddenly, things turned sour. Jesus was arrested, and Peter the Rock got scared. Under pressure, he crumbled, and on that fateful night, he denied his Lord three times. The next day, Good Friday, Jesus was nailed to a cross, and Simon Peter was devastated—shattered, defeated, brokenhearted.

But then came Easter, and Simon Peter was thrilled beyond belief, excited, gratified about Christ's resurrection. But he was still confused and perplexed about his own future and also ashamed of his past failure. So Peter returns to Galilee with his friends; several days pass and nothing happens.

Finally, in typical fashion, Simon Peter gets impatient. He can't take it anymore, and with a tone of agitation, he announces, "I'm going fishing!" Now, what Simon means is this: "I can't handle this any longer. This waiting around is driving me up a wall. I'm worn out with the indecision, the waiting, the risk involved. I don't know about the rest of you, but I'm going fishing. I'm going back to the old secure life, the old life of being a fisherman."

The others go along with him. They fish all night but

have no luck. But then as dawn breaks, they see someone standing on the shore. It's the Risen Lord, but they don't recognize him at this point. He tells them to cast their nets on the right side of the boat. They do—and bring in a huge catch, 153 large fish.

The lightbulb comes on for the disciple called John, and he turns and says to Peter, "It's the Lord!" And Simon Peter, always excitable and impulsive, dives in and swims urgently to shore. The others come in on the boat, and as they come ashore, they see the Risen Christ cooking breakfast for them (another Holy Communion). He takes Simon Peter off to the side, and three times, he asks him the same question, "Simon, do you love me?" And when Simon Peter answers, "Yes, Lord, you know that I love you," the Risen Lord says to him, "Feed my sheep!"

Of course, it's obvious here that Christ is forgiving Peter and giving him a chance to profess his love three times, to make up for his earlier threefold denial.

Then the story ends exactly the way it started months before, with Christ saying to Simon at the seashore these powerful words: "Follow me."

Isn't that a great story—jam-packed with the stuff of life: powerful symbols, strong emotions, dramatic lessons. See how the Risen Christ seeks out Simon Peter and meets his need, and he does that for us too. He seeks us out and meets our needs. In Simon Peter's experience with him back then, we get a practical glimpse at the powerful ways the Risen Christ meets and helps us today. Let's look together at this great promise—the promise of God's presence with us.

When We Need Encouragement, He Is There

If ever anybody needed encouragement, it was Simon Peter in that moment. He was down. He felt like a failure. He was defeated and ashamed. In the crisis of Holy

Week, on that Thursday night when Jesus was arrested, Peter had denied his Master. His failure was magnified, because only moments before, he had bragged loudly about his unswerving loyalty.

When Jesus and the disciples had completed their last supper in the upper room, they had gone out to the Mount of Olives, and there Jesus had said to them, "The time is near, and you will all fall away. You will all desert me."

"Oh no!" cried Simon Peter. "Not I! Even though all the others may fall away, I will not. I will never desert you. I will stand with you to the end. You can count on me."

But Jesus said to him, "This day, this very night, before the cock crows twice, you will deny me three times" (Mark 14:30).

"No! No!" Simon Peter insisted vehemently. "I will never deny you. I will never forsake you. I would die with you first!"

Well, we know the rest of the story, don't we? Under intense pressure, Simon Peter caved in and denied his Lord. And being the bold personality he was, that failure crushed him. He was down for the count. And now, even though he had witnessed the resurrection, deep down inside, Simon still was feeling the anguish and agony of his own personal failure.

In that fateful moment, on that Thursday night before Good Friday, he had lost his courage, lost his nerve, lost his strength and bravado. Peter, the Rock, had crumbled, and now he felt like dirt! But then along came the Risen Christ to give him the encouragement he needed so much.

It's important to remember that the word *encourage* literally means "to put the heart in." The word *discourage* means "to tear the heart out." In John 21, we see Christ graciously putting the heart back into Simon Peter, giving him encouragement. No stern lectures here.

No blame placing or finger pointing here—just words of encouragement.

The Risen Christ is saying, "I still love you. I still believe in you. I still trust you, and I want you to take up the torch of my ministry. I want you to take care of my sheep." These words of encouragement were the wake-up call Simon Peter needed, and as we read on in the Scriptures, we see that he became one of the courageous leaders and martyrs of the early church.

The Risen Christ came to Simon Peter that morning with words of encouragement, and when we need encouragement, he will be there for us as well. If we would hear those words and respond to them in faith, as Peter did, we could turn this world upside down.

When We Need Forgiveness, He Is There

Simon Peter needed forgiveness, and that is precisely what Christ came to give him.

A minister friend of mine recently shared with me a true story which underscores the power of forgiveness. It happened some years ago. A young man we will call Eli, a member of his church, pulled into a service station, and while there, he became involved in an altercation with an older man, a fellow church member. The older man had been drinking and tried to pick a fight with Eli.

Later the young man said, "I don't know why I didn't just get in my car and drive away. I had been fussed at and cussed before. But he just kept on and on, and I lost control and I pushed him."

The older man, in his drunken state, fell over a curb when he was pushed, hit his head on a concrete bench, and fell dead. Well, as you can imagine, it traumatized the whole town. Everybody knew everybody in that little village, and as the word spread, people began to choose up sides. Tension was crackling in the air.

My minister friend received a call from Eli, who said, "Reverend, I've got to go see his wife. Will you go with me? If you don't want to be seen with me, I understand. But I have to go and tell her how sorry I am."

The minister and Eli went to the home of the older man to see his widow. As they walked up, people were everywhere—in the yard, on the porch, in the living room and the kitchen, and no one spoke to them. When the recently widowed woman heard they were there, she called them into the back room. Eli was scared to death, but he was ready to tell her how sorry he was. He never got to make his speech.

As soon as she saw him, she ran to him, took his hands in hers, and said, "Eli, I have known you all your life. I remember the night you were born. I know you didn't do it on purpose." Then she hugged him and healed him— and with that hug, she healed the whole town!

Now, where did she learn the kind of compassion and forgiveness? You know, don't you? She learned it at church. She learned it from Jesus Christ! That's what Christ was doing for Simon Peter on the seashore that morning long ago. He was giving him the healing hug of forgiveness. And he has a hug like that for you and me. When we need encouragement and when we need forgiveness, he is there.

When We Need Direction, He Is There

Simon Peter and the other disciples had been waiting around, wondering, "What next? What are we supposed to do now?" Then the Risen Christ came to give them a new direction.

He said, "If you love me, feed my sheep." What he meant was, "Take up the torch of my ministry! Go! Be the church for this needy world!" The world is starving for Jesus Christ, and we have him. Our task is to feed his sheep, share him with others.

I have a good friend who is one of the finest Christians I have ever known. Dedicated, capable, effective, one of

the most respected churchmen in America today. He
grew up in a Methodist parsonage, but he tells us that at
one point, when he was a young man, he drifted away
from the church.

During that period, he fell in love with a beautiful
young woman. He asked her to go on a Sunday morning
picnic with him.

I love her response: "If you want to be with me on
Sunday morning, we will be together in church!" Well,
he wanted to be with her, so he went with her to church
that Sunday morning, and they have hardly missed a
Sunday since.

She brought him back to God and to the church. She
knew how to take up the torch, how to share Christ, how
to feed his sheep. And God's church has been blessed
by this great couple ever since—all because she had a
sense of God's direction and the courage to go in God's
direction.

The Risen Christ is here with us right now. He has
some incredible promises and some special gifts for us.
Won't you receive them? Won't you accept them? He
promises to be with us in every circumstance of life, and
he promises to give us encouragement, forgiveness, and
direction.

3

The Promise of a Rock-Solid Foundation

Building on the Rock

MATTHEW 7:21, 24-27

"Not everyone who says to me, 'Lord, Lord,' will enter the kingdom of heaven, but only the one who does the will of my Father in heaven.... Everyone then who hears these words of mine and acts on them will be like a wise man who built his house on rock. The rain fell, the floods came, and the winds blew and beat on that house, but it did not fall, because it had been founded on rock. And everyone who hears these words of mine and does not act on them will be like a foolish man who built his house on sand. The rain fell, and the floods came, and the winds blew and beat against that house, and it fell—and great was its fall."

Some years ago, in a small town in Central Europe, a visitor saw something that fascinated him—something that seemed very strange to him. He noticed all the native villagers performing the same highly unusual ritual. As they passed by a certain ordinary looking wall, they would nod casually in the direction of the wall, then make the sign of the cross as they walked on by.

Some would be walking briskly, others more slowly, but they all did the same thing. They would nod at the wall and make the sign of the cross as they passed by. When the visitor asked why they did this, no one knew. "We've always done that," they said. "It's a tradition, a time-honored ritual in our village. Everybody does it! Always have!"

The visitor's curiosity got the best of him and he began chipping away at the layers of whitewash and dirt that covered the wall until, underneath the grime, he discovered a magnificent mural of Mary and the baby Jesus! Generations before, the townspeople had had a beautiful reason for bowing and making the sign of the cross at that place. It had been an altar of prayer in the heart of the village.

But succeeding generations didn't know that. They had only learned the ritual. They continued to go through the motions without knowing the reason behind them. They performed the practice, but it had absolutely no meaning for them and made no impact on their lives at all. That's an appropriate parable for many people today, in their approach to religion, isn't it?

Their faith experience is not much more than a vague nod in God's direction. They casually perform some of the rituals of faith, but they don't really know why. And the rituals have become so routine, so casual, so matter-of-fact, that there is no power, no strength, no inspiration in them at all—a little nod here, a token gesture there, but no depth, no spirit, no life!

But in the Sermon on the Mount, Jesus shows us dramatically that this kind of shallow, nonchalant approach to faith won't work. There are storms ahead—the rains of trouble will fall, the floods of stress will come, the winds of challenge will lash against us. Shaky, unstable, wavering, casual routine faith won't hold together. The storms of life will rip it apart and smash it to the ground. We need a strong and stable house of faith, built on a rock-solid foundation!

Here's how Jesus put it. He said: "Not everyone who says to me, 'Lord, Lord,' [i.e., not everyone who makes a casual nod in my direction] will enter the kingdom of heaven, but only the one who does the will of my Father in heaven.... Everyone then who hears these words of mine and acts on them will be like a wise man who built his house on rock. The rain fell, the floods came, and the winds blew and beat on that house, but it did not fall, because it had been founded on rock."

Now, what is this rock-solid foundation that Jesus is talking about? What are the promises? Well, this is the conclusion of the Sermon on the Mount, and he is obviously referring to what he has just taught in the preceding chapters. As a matter of fact, he says that: "Hear these words and do them, and you will be wise and strong, but if you hear these words and don't do them, you will be foolish and weak."

Now, when we go back and read through the Sermon on the Mount carefully, we discover several recurring and dominant themes. Let me underscore three of them.

First, There Is Rock-Solid Commitment

All through the Sermon on the Mount, there is the call to commitment: "Be peacemakers"; "Let your light shine"; "Enter the narrow gate."

Let me ask you: Do you have a rock-solid commitment? How would you rate your commitment to Christ? On a scale of one to ten, with ten being absolutely terrific and one being very poor, how would you rate your commitment to God and the church?

Do you really put God first in your life? Do you really love God with all your heart, soul, mind, and strength? Are you really committed to God's kingdom, and to the doing of God's will? Are you really committed to living daily in the Spirit of Christ? Do you really love that person next to you right now as much as you love yourself?

Are you wholeheartedly committed to supporting and upholding the church with your prayers, your presence, your gifts, and your service?

At the conclusion of the Sermon on the Mount, Jesus points out vividly that a commitment built on shaky, shifting sands will not work. A rock-solid commitment is needed. An unflinching, unwavering commitment to Christ is what we must have to stand against the treacherous storms of life.

Some years ago, I received a call one morning from some dear friends. "We've just received the results of Mom's tests," they said. "It's bad news—real bad. She has six months to a year to live, and we want you to come and tell her the situation." She was fifty-seven years old. She was at home, and when I got there, she was seated by the window in the den, watching her granddaughter playing in the backyard. As I sat down with her, I was trying to figure out how to say it, how to tell her. And the following conversation took place.

"Well, Jim," she said, "It looks like you drew the short straw. I know you've come to give me the bad news."

"Well," I answered, "I do have the results of your tests."

"How long do I have?" she asked.

"Now, you know it's hard to be precise on these things, but the doctors say six months to a year."

"I'm not surprised," she said. "That's about what I expected."

We were quiet for a moment, and then I asked, "How do you feel inside right now?"

She said, "When I look out there and see my granddaughter, I feel like crying." And I told her I felt like crying too, and we did cry a little, but then she went on, "Jim, I'm not afraid. All my life I've gone to Sunday school and church. I'm a believer! I'm committed to Christ with every fiber of my being. Christ has been my Savior in this life. He will be my Savior in the life to come. I believe that with all my heart, and I'm committed to him heart and soul!"

Now, let me ask you: Are you committed to Christ like that? Is your commitment that strong? That woman had built her life on the solid rock of commitment. She trusted God's promises, and when the storm came, that rock-solid commitment served her well.

Second, There Is Rock-Solid Trust

This, too, is a prominent theme in the Sermon on the Mount: "Don't be anxious. Don't be fretful. Don't be afraid. Just seek first God's Kingdom and righteousness. Let God rule in your life. Trust God, and things will fall in place for you." What a promise!

The artist Rembrandt once painted a canvas titled "Storm on the Sea of Galilee." It's a remarkable work of art for two reasons.

1. After all, it's a Rembrandt, a priceless masterpiece, a portrayal so real you can almost feel the spray of the waves and the movement of the boat.

2. But this painting is striking for another unique reason. As you study the detail, you notice something unusual: There are fourteen men on the boat. Now, wait a minute—weren't there twelve disciples? You count again, and yes—there are thirteen men, plus Jesus, on the boat—a total of fourteen.

Gradually, your eyes focus on one particular figure. He is holding on for dear life. Suddenly, you recognize the face. It's the face of Rembrandt! The artist has painted himself into the scene. He is experiencing the storm, and it's frightful—but the good news is: Jesus is there! Jesus is in the boat with him. Jesus will save him from the fury of the storm!

The Apostle Paul expressed it like this: "I am ready for anything, for Christ is with me and he is my strength." Do you have that kind of faith? Do you know that kind of trust?

William McElvaney once described an interesting happening during the communion service in his church one Sunday morning. It was a small church, and the congregation had been instructed to pass the elements down the pew, with each person saying the words of administration to the next: "John, this is the body of our Lord given for you; John, this is the blood of our Lord shed for you."

But on this day, one man in the congregation who was not especially liturgically minded turned to his neighbor, handed him the bread, and promptly forgot what he was supposed to say. He just went blank. After a brief but agonizing pause, he finally blurted out these words: "Harvey—Hang in there!"

I've seen a number of different liturgies for the Lord's Supper over the years, and I don't really think the words "Harvey, hang in there" are in any of them. But the truth is that I can't think of any better words to say when we are remembering Christ's gift to us, his presence with us, his care over us. What better words could you say than those—"hang in there!" You can "hang in there" with rock-solid commitment, and rock-solid trust, and he will see you through. You can count on that! It's a divine promise.

Third, There Is Rock-Solid Love

Jesus calls for love in a powerful way in the Sermon on the Mount: "Love your enemies ... pray for those who persecute you ... be perfectly loving, as God is."

John and Margie were married back in 1941. Both of them were rugged people, raised on the farmlands of America. Together, they had big dreams, high hopes of becoming the most successful farmers in the United States.

However, four years after they were married, and after two children were born, Margie was struck down with polio. She spent the rest of her life in an iron lung. Still so young—they were just in their twenties—their life dreams were shattered. There was no one to keep the house going, no one to raise the children, no one to be a real partner with John, no one to share his bed.

John had to give up his lifelong dream of farming and devote his life to taking care of Margie and the children. Many years later, when John and Margie celebrated their fortieth wedding anniversary, someone asked John how he had done it all those years. John answered simply, "I'm a Christian, and we try to keep our promises. And besides, I love her."

A few years later, after Margie died, their son asked John how he had done it all those years. Again, John's answer was simple: "I never thought about doing anything else. You just do it, and God helps you."

(Thanks to Don Shelby for this illustration.)

You know where John learned that kind of sacrificial love, don't you? He learned it at the church. He learned it in the Scriptures. He learned it in the Sermon on the Mount. He learned it at Golgotha. He learned it from Jesus, the King of Love.

If you and I will just do it—just build our lives on rock-solid commitment, on rock-solid trust, on rock-solid love—then God promises to help us. God promises to be with us and give us strength. God promises to hold us together, to enable us to withstand the treacherous, dangerous storms of life. God will be our firm foundation. That's a promise on which we can stand, tall and secure and confident.

4

The Promise of Peace

Give Peace a Chance

MATTHEW 5:9

"Blessed are the peacemakers, for they will be called children of God."

A few years ago, a little six-year-old boy named Tommy Tighe showed up at the Children's Bank in Huntington Beach, California, and asked to speak to the Chief Executive Officer. Tommy shook hands with the CEO, Mark Victor Hansen, and said, "My name is Tommy Tighe. I'm six years old, and I want to borrow some money from your Children's Bank."

The CEO smiled and said, "Well, Tommy, that's what we do. We loan money to kids. And so far, all the kids have paid the money back. Tell me, how much do you need, and what do you want to do?"

Tommy answered. "Ever since I was four years old, I've had a vision that I could cause peace in the world. I want to make a bumper sticker that says PEACE, PLEASE! DO IT FOR US KIDS! and signed Tommy. I need $454 to produce 1,000 bumper stickers."

The loan was approved, the check was issued, and Tommy moved forward with his Peace Plan. He sent bumper stickers to the presidents and leaders of nations all over the world—to the White House, to the Kremlin, to Buckingham Palace, and many many other places. He persuaded his dad to drive him up to Ronald Reagan's home so that he could hand deliver a bumper sticker to the former president. And while they were waiting at the front gate, he sold one to Mr. Reagan's gatekeeper.

Mikhail Gorbachev, the President of the USSR at the time, wrote back to Tommy and sent a check for $1.50 to pay for his bumper sticker. He also included a picture that said: "Go For Peace, Tommy!" and signed it Mikhail Gorbachev, President.

A newspaper reporter who interviewed Tommy about his work for peace asked him, "Tommy, do you really think you can bring world peace?"

Tommy answered, "I don't think I am quite old enough yet. I'm only six, and I think you have to be eight or nine to stop all the wars in the world."

Tommy went on the Joan Rivers show and wowed Joan, the camera crew, the live and television audiences. He was so interesting, so authentic, so persuasive that the members of the studio audience began pulling out their money to buy Tommy's "PEACE, PLEASE! DO IT FOR US KIDS" bumper stickers on the spot.

At the end of the program, Joan Rivers said, "Tommy, do you really think you can make a difference? Do you really think your bumper sticker can bring peace to our world?"

I love Tommy's answer: "So far I've had it out two years and got the Berlin Wall down. I'm doing pretty good, don't you think?"

(Adapted from Jack Canfield and Mark Victor Hansen, *Chicken Soup for the Soul* [Deerfield Beach, Fla.: Health Communications, Inc., 1993], pp. 173-76.)

Thanks to Tommy and others like him, crying out from the grassroots, things became better on the world scene. The Berlin Wall came down. The Iron Curtain came down. The Cold War thawed, and Eastern Europe opened up. But sadly, now the battleground has shifted—

the battlefield has come to our own backyard. Our streets, our schools, our courtrooms have become war zones. Just when we found ourselves thinking that at long last, maybe the decade of the 90s will be a decade of peace, we have suddenly realized, through a crescendo of traumatic events, that war has sprung up in our very own neighborhoods.

Think about our streets. John Hart, Jr., was an outstanding military officer. He served with distinction and courage in the Persian Gulf War. He dodged bullets, Scud missiles and machine-gun fire. He was a Desert Storm hero. But shortly after returning safely home, he was cut down and killed in a blaze of bullets—a result of street-gang violence as he stood in front of his parents' home on the west side of Chicago.

Or how about Anthony Riggs? He was twenty-two years old when he returned from the Persian Gulf crisis on March 8, 1991. Ten days later, on March 18, he was loading a van to help his family move when he was shot. The gunman escaped in a stolen car. Anthony Riggs died there on the street, in front of his home in Detroit. It was learned later that his own family had taken out a large insurance policy on Anthony prior to his departure for the Persian Gulf. When he returned home from war safely, a member of his family shot him to death, in hope of collecting the insurance money. Our streets have become a new battlefield.

And think about our schools. When Dr. Rod Paige was superintendent of the Houston Independent School District, he put it in perspective when he said his number-one priority as he went into office was not education, but security in the schools and safety for the students. He said, and he is right, "You can't do much educating when the children are frightened and scared and anxious about their own safety. We have to fix that first."

Indeed so. When students must walk through a metal detector to get into school; when children literally are afraid to go into a school restroom during the school day; when children are susceptible to being shot or approached by drug dealers as they walk to and from school, something is terribly wrong, and we have to address that. Dr. Paige is right: We have to fix that first!

And what about our courtrooms—talk about battle-fields! Just think of all the things that have been in the news in recent times—neighbors, friends, coworkers, family members, going after one another in the courts. It's unbelievable! There is something I have been want-ing to say for a long time—and I'm going to say it now.

In my opinion, one of the greatest problems we have in America today is that we have become too litigation-minded! People sue one another at the drop of a hat—and it is absolutely eating us up as a nation. It is driving the cost of living out of sight! I saw a bumper sticker recent-ly that put it like this: FAIRNESS YES ... GREED NO ... STOP LAWSUIT ABUSE.

Our streets, our schools, our courtrooms have become the new "battle zones," and we must find a way to bring peace to these trouble spots. We need Tommy's bumper sticker right here at home—PEACE, PLEASE! DO IT FOR US KIDS! But even more, we need the counsel and witness of Jesus. Remember what he said: "Blessed are the peacemakers, for they will be called children of God." What he meant was this: "Yes, you! I want you to be a peacemaker. There is nothing in the world you can do that will please me more. Peacemaking is what it's all about. It is the most godlike thing you can do!"

Peacemaking is the very height of spiritual maturity. Childish people want to fight. Spiritually mature people want to heal. Childish people build walls. Spiritually mature people build bridges. Childish people recoil and resent. Spiritually mature people restore and reconcile. Please notice the way this Beatitude ends. Jesus said, "The peacemakers . . . will be called children of God." That's very significant, because in the Bible, whenever we see the words "sons of God" or "daughters of God" or "children of God," that means GODLIKE—those who have within them the attributes and qualities of God. What a unique and beautiful promise this is!

So when we read that the peacemakers will be called "children of God," it means, *"Blessed are the peacemakers, for they are doing a godlike work."* Nothing is more godly than the act of peacemaking. If you want to "make happy" the heart of God, live in that spirit! Be a reconciler. Imitate God's redemptive, peacemaking ways, and you will be called a child of God. That's a promise!

One of the things that fascinates me about sports is the way the coaches position their players. Close games are often won or lost, a particular play can succeed or fail, because of the placement of the players. It's true in all sports that positioning is all-important! It is tremendously important, too, in the game of life. And in this seventh Beatitude, in Matthew 5:9, Jesus is saying to us, "Here's your position! Go into life as peacemakers! Let that be your stance. Let that be your attitude, your approach, your commitment. Take the position of peacemakers!"

Now, let me underscore three specific ways we can be peacemakers today.

First, We Can Make Peace with Ourselves

There is a beautiful hymn with these words: "Let there be peace on earth and let it begin with me." More and more these days, psychologists are telling us how important it is to be at peace within, at peace with ourselves, to feel good about who we are, to have a healthy sense of self-esteem. Those who have good self-esteem—those who are at peace within—are the ones most likely to be loving, productive, caring, creative, helpful, happy people. And those who have poor self-esteem—those who are at war within—are the ones most likely to have

45

problems with drugs, problems with other people, problems with family members, problems with the law. To compensate for their poor self-image (and the civil war going on inside) they take drugs, join gangs, carry guns, because they don't feel capable of facing life without some crutch.

Some years ago a man came to the church for help. "Everything's gone wrong," he said. "I have lost confidence in my professional ability. My wife has left me. I can't get along with my children. I'm cut off from my parents and my in-laws. I'm having conflicts with my coworkers. I've been drinking heavily. Everybody has left me, and I don't blame them. I've been bitter and hostile. I've done so many mean and cruel things . . . and now I have so many problems." He paused and took a deep breath. Then he leaned forward and said, "To tell you the truth, I think all those problems are really symptoms. My real problem is that I don't like myself, and that taints everything I touch and do."

Well, he was probably right. When you are at war within, it smudges and distorts every relationship. Whenever we encounter a person who is continually bitter, critical, always complaining, perpetually finding fault, repeatedly doing selfish, greedy, cruel things that wound and hurt, we can be sure that we are dealing with someone who does not like himself or herself, someone who is not at peace within. That seething, brooding bitterness is merely a projection of his or her own self-contempt.

Now, let me ask you: Do you want to feel good about yourself? Do you want to like yourself more? Do you want to be at peace within? Then remember this: You are special to God. You are valuable to God. You are precious to God. You are so important to God that he gave his only Son for you.

That's the first way we can be peacemakers today—we can make peace with ourselves.

Second, We Can Make Peace with Other People

We don't have to be at war with others. A few years ago, the Special Olympics were held in Seattle, and a beautiful thing happened. Nine contestants, all with physical or mental disabilities, stood at the starting line for the 100-yard dash. As the gun sounded, they all started out—not exactly in a dash, but with a relish to run the race to the finish and win. But as they ran, one boy slipped and fell. He tumbled over a couple of times and began to cry. The other eight runners heard the boy crying. They all stopped, turned around and went back— every one of them.

One girl with Down's Syndrome bent down and kissed him on top of his head, and said, "This will make it all better." The other runners helped the fallen boy up, and all nine of them linked arms and walked together, side by side, to the finish line. They all won! They all came in first! Everyone in the stadium stood, and the cheering went on for ten minutes. People who were there are still telling the story. People who weren't even there say they were.

Why? Because deep down, we know this one thing: What matters in this life is not just winning for yourself. What truly matters is helping others win, even if it sometimes means slowing yourself down and changing your course.

(*Homiletics*, Oct.–Dec., 1993, p. 5)

Do you need to slow yourself down and change your course to make peace with somebody? Do you need to reconcile with someone? Are you at war with anybody? If so, now is the time to fix it, now is the time to make it right, now is the time to make peace. You may say, "It's not my fault." Of course it's not your fault, but if you are a Christian, it is your responsibility to reach out in peace, to be a peacemaker. You don't have to win. Just go fix it. Go make peace with others.

Third, We Can Make Peace with God

That's how the old-timers used to say it: "Have you made your peace with God?" They knew that God is the Prince of Peace, that he is the Savior, the Reconciler, the Redeemer, the One who reaches out to us, the One who delivers and restores. But they also knew that we must do our part; we must accept his acceptance! In faith, we must receive him into our hearts and into our lives, and commit ourselves in service to him.

Have you heard about the man who boarded an airplane one evening? When the flight attendant asked if he would like dinner, he asked, "What are my choices?" She answered, "Yes or No!" When it comes to God, those are our choices—Yes or No. We can't sit on the fence, can't skirt the issue. We have to decide—Yes or No. Do we accept God into our lives, or not? Do we commit our lives to him, or not?

The powerful Emperor Charlemagne made an unusual request regarding his burial. He asked to be buried sitting upright on his throne, with his crown on his head, his scepter in his hand, his royal cape draped around his shoulders, with an open book placed on his lap. That was in A.D. 814. Nearly two hundred years later, Emperor Othello wanted to see whether Charlemagne's burial request had indeed been carried out. He ordered that the tomb be opened.

They found the body placed just as Charlemagne had requested. Only now, nearly two centuries later, the scene was gruesome. The crown was tilted on the skeletal head. The scepter was tarnished. The cape was moth-eaten, the body disfigured. But there, open on his lap, was the book Charlemagne had requested—the Bible! And one bony finger pointed to Matthew 16:26: "What is a man profited, if he shall gain the whole world, and lose his own soul?" (KJV).

Well, how is it with you? Are you at peace with yourself? Are you at peace with other people? Are you at peace with God? If not, why don't you give peace a chance? Our Lord is the Prince of Peace. He wants to give us peace within. He promised that. And he wants us to pass it on to others. He wants us to be peacemakers.

5

The Promise of Victory

From Victims to Victors

2 CORINTHIANS 4:8-14

We are afflicted in every way, but not crushed; perplexed, but not driven to despair; persecuted, but not forsaken; struck down, but not destroyed; always carrying in the body the death of Jesus, so that the life of Jesus may also be made visible in our bodies. For while we live, we are always being given up to death for Jesus' sake, so that the life of Jesus may be made visible in our mortal flesh. So death is at work in us, but life in you.

But just as we have the same spirit of faith that is in accordance with scripture—"I believed, and so I spoke"—we also believe, and so we speak, because we know that the one who raised the Lord Jesus will raise us also with Jesus, and will bring us with you into his presence.

Many of you are familiar with the "Calvin and Hobbes" comic strip. For those who may not be aware of these delightful cartoon characters, let me explain the set-up. Calvin is a precocious little boy who has a beloved stuffed tiger named Hobbes. They are inseparable. When adults are around, Hobbes remains a small stuffed tiger, but when Calvin and Hobbes are alone,

Hobbes becomes a larger than life imaginary friend for Calvin. Calvin and Hobbes have the most interesting adventures, experiences, and conversations. Some months ago, the comic strip depicted Calvin and Hobbes walking together in the snow. Calvin, the little boy, begins to philosophize, reasoning that whenever he does something wrong, it is not really his fault. Society is to blame. Here's how he put it: "Nothing I do is my fault. My family is dysfunctional. And my parents won't empower me! Consequently, I'm not self-actualized! My behavior is addictive, functioning in a disease process of toxic codependency! I need holistic healing and wellness before I will accept any responsibility for any of my actions!"

Then, with a smile, he adds, "I love the Culture of Victimhood! It's great, because you can always find somebody to blame things on!"

Then Hobbes, the tiger, says, "One of us needs to stick his head in a bucket of ice water!"

In this comic strip, Calvin has expressed a disturbing notion that is pervading our country just now—a notion that, in some instances, is understandable. But the truth is that, in most instances, it is suspect and dangerous. I'm talking about the troublesome notion that goes something like this: "Society has oppressed me, so I have a right to lash out in hostility." "Society has mistreated me, so I am justified in seeking my revenge." "Society has cheated me, so you owe me." "Society has been unfair to me, so if I do something wrong, it's not really my fault. I'm not responsible."

Many people today are embracing, adopting, and encouraging this thought process, this philosophy of life that Calvin called the Culture of Victimhood.

Some years ago in New York, a violent criminal attacked, mugged, and almost killed a seventy-two-year-old man. A policeman came on the scene, and in the process of making the arrest, a scuffle broke out. The mugger was shot. Later, the mugger sued the city, citing the ways society had failed him and protesting the fact that he had been shot by a policeman. Are you ready for this? The mugger was awarded $4.3 million! What was the public reaction? Virtual silence.

During the 1992 Los Angeles riots, some men were filmed jerking an innocent man out of his truck, bashing his skull with a brick, hitting and kicking him repeatedly, and then doing a victory dance over his fallen body. Subsequently, the attackers were arrested, but they argued that they should not be held accountable for the attack, because they were caught up in mob violence, mob madness. "They were found not guilty on most counts … and the sound you heard throughout the land was relief," according to William J. Bennett in the *Wall Street Journal* (December 10, 1993).

And in the Midwest, a college professor was once sued by a student. Why? Because the student failed a course! The student said that the professor violated his rights and negatively affected his future by giving him a failing grade. The student said that he was born into a dysfunctional family, and consequently did not receive the help and encouragement he needed at home during his formative years. So society had failed him, and therefore his failing grade was not really his fault!

This "culture of victimhood" mind-set is not just out there in society. It is also highly prevalent in the counseling room. So many people today are the shackled and paralyzed victims of some past event, past situation, past decision, or past relationship. They are crying out for someone to free them from "the tyranny of their past."

That's why the Christian faith is so important and so relevant—because that is precisely where Jesus Christ can help and heal. He can set us free! He can give us new life! He can make us victors, rather than victims. He comes into our lives, saying, "Follow me!" And anyone who says "Follow me" is obviously more interested in the future than in the past. Jesus certainly is. With Jesus, it's not where you've been, but where you're going; not whether you have fallen, but whether you will get up; not the skeletons of your past, but the promise and hope for the future.

In recent years, a new approach to psychiatry called Reality Therapy has emerged. Its founding mentor was a man named William Glasser. The approach is a little blunt, but it makes sense to me. Reality therapists will not let us spend a lot of time rummaging around in the past. Rather, they say, "So, you've had a problem? You've had it rough? You've been hurt? So what? Everybody has problems. Now, what are you going to do about it?"

It is remarkable to note in the Bible how little time Jesus spent talking with people about their past. He was more interested in their future. When the woman taken in adultery was brought to him, he did not explore the circumstances that had pushed her to her fall. He simply took her by the hand, lifted her up, and said, "Neither do I condemn you. Go your way, and from now on do not sin again" (John 8:11b).

And when Nicodemus came to him under the cover of night, shackled by an impossible legalism, Jesus didn't ask him how he got that way or fuss at him for being that way, but simply said to him, "No one can see the kingdom of God without being born from above" (John 3:3b).

Then nowhere is it more beautifully depicted for us than in his parable of the prodigal son. The father doesn't even let the prodigal finish his confession—doesn't want to hear it. He wants to get on with the party.

This, too, is the good news of our Christian faith for you and me. We don't have to be defeated by the hurts or problems or failures or sins of the past.

We can make a new beginning; we can have a new life. We don't have to be victims. We can be victors.

This is what the Apostle Paul is talking about in his letters to the Corinthian Christians. He describes his hardships and troubles, and how he has been victimized, but he does not see himself as a victim. Rather, he ends with a victorious crescendo of praise to God:

Five times I have received ... the forty lashes minus one.
Three times I was beaten with rods. Once I received a
stoning. Three times I was shipwrecked; for a night and a
day I was adrift at sea; on frequent journeys, in danger
from rivers, danger from bandits, danger from my own
people, danger from Gentiles, danger in the city, danger in
the wilderness, danger at sea, danger from false brothers
and sisters; in toil and hardship, through many a sleepless
night, hungry and thirsty, often without food, cold and
naked.... The governor under King Aretas guarded the
city of Damascus in order to seize me, but I was let down
in a basket through a window in the wall, and escaped
from his hands. (2 Cor. 11:24-27, 32-33)

But after all that, Paul did not give up. He did not quit.
He did not waver. Rather, he said, triumphantly:

We are afflicted in every way, but not crushed; perplexed,
but not driven to despair; persecuted, but not forsaken;
struck down, but not destroyed.... So we do not lose
heart. (2 Cor. 4:8-9, 16a)
For we know that if the earthly tent we live in is
destroyed, we have a building from God, a house not
made with hands, eternal in the heavens. (2 Cor. 5:1)
"Where, O death, is your victory? Where, O death, is
your sting?" ... But thanks be to God, who gives us the
victory through our Lord Jesus Christ. (1 Cor. 15:55, 57)

This is the good news of the Christian faith. You can
rise above it all! What an incredible promise! By the
grace of God and the power of God—the presence of
God—you don't have to be a victim anymore. You can be
a victor! Let me show you how.

With the Help of God, You Can Rise Above Your Circumstances

I remember an old story about a family who had twin
boys. One son grew up and became an alcoholic. When

someone asked him why, he said, "Because of my father!"

The other son grew up and became a minister, and he dedicated his ministry to working with and helping alcoholics. When someone asked him why, he said, "Because of my father!" The two sons grew up in exactly the same environment. One was trapped, shackled, paralyzed, pulled down by his situation. The other turned to God and rose above it all.

Sometimes we hear people say, "I'm doing the best I can under the circumstances." Well, we don't have to live *under* the circumstances. By the grace of God, we can rise *above* them. We don't need to remain victims. God can make us victors.

We know that with the help of God, we can rise above our circumstances.

With the Help of God, You Can Rise Above Your Defeats

Before Johnny Cash was thirty years old, his country songs had made him one of the most popular men on the American entertainment scene. But unfortunately, Johnny Cash started taking pep pills, then antidepressants, and before he knew it, he had become a drug addict. At times, he was taking as many as 100 pills a day. Then one morning, somewhere in Georgia, he woke up and realized that he was in jail. He didn't know how he got there. He didn't remember a thing. But this had happened before. He was in jail again.

The jailer told him, "Johnny, one of the night men found you stumbling around the streets. We only brought you in so you wouldn't hurt yourself. You're doing time right now, Johnny, the worst kind. I'm a big fan of yours. I've always admired you. It's a shame to see you ruining yourself like this. I didn't know you were this bad off." He shook his head sadly and continued, "I don't know where you think you got your talent from, Johnny, but if you think it came from God, like I do, then you sure are wrecking the body he put it in."

With that, the jailer opened the cell door and let Johnny Cash go free. It was the turning point.

Later, he said, "Someday, I am going back to Georgia and find that jailer and thank him and shake his hand. He saved my life. That morning, as I stepped out into the warm sunshine, I took a good, hard look at my life, and I knew that I was a better man than the one I had become.

"It was that reference to God that suddenly cleared my mind, because until that morning it hadn't occurred to me to turn to God for help in kicking my habit. Suddenly I realized that I would need all the power I could get, and I knew this power could come only from God. I asked him to go to work on me then and there, and he did. He saved me. He turned my life around. He set me free."

(Adapted from Norman Vincent Peale, "You Are Invincible," *Plus: The Magazine of Positive Thinking*, the Peale Center for Christian Living.)

I don't know what defeats and heartaches and problems you are grappling with right now, but I do know one thing: You need all the power you can get, and that power comes only from God. God can save you. God can turn it around for you. God can set you free. That's God's promise. God can empower you to rise above your circumstances and above your defeats.

With the Help of God, You Can Rise Above Your Despair

Sometimes when you are in the valleys of life, you feel so down that you can see no way out. But if you will walk with God one step at a time, one day at a time, God will bring you out of the valley to the mountaintop.

A few years ago, an elderly Englishman, a man in his

eighties, described the horrible bombing of London a half century ago. It was one of the worst and most frightening times ever experienced by the British people. At the time of the bombing, this man was in his early thirties. He recalled how horrified he was as he stood on the outskirts of London and watched the central city go up in smoke. Bomb after bomb fell, one building after another burst into flames. The sky was filled with black smoke as far as he could see.

With tears in his eyes, the older man said, "It seemed to me at that moment that everything was lost—the war, England, all the values of civilization. I found myself asking again and again, 'It there any hope?' I was filled with despair. I found myself crying like a baby. Then an amazing thing happened. There was a sudden gust of wind for just a moment. It blew the smoke away just long enough for me to see the cross of Christ atop the dome of St. Paul's Cathedral. And the instant I saw it, I felt a great surge of hope. And I stopped crying, because I knew—I really knew as never before—that there is a power greater than all the power of evil, a power that cannot be defeated, a power that would see us through—a power that would live on."

That is the good news of our faith, isn't it?—symbolized in the cross! God wins! Nothing can defeat God. And God promises to share the victory with us. We don't have to be victims anymore. We can be victors! That's what Jesus came to show us. That's what Paul believed. We can believe it, too, and when we do, it sets us free! It resurrects us—raises us above our circumstances, above our defeats, above our despair. That's good news! It's the greatest news ever heard—and the greatest promise ever given! The promise of victory!

6

The Promise of Conversion

Turning Inkblots into Angels

ROMANS 8:28, 31, 35, 37-39

We know that all things work together for good for those who love God, who are called according to his purpose.... What then are we to say about these things? If God is for us, who is against us? ... Who will separate us from the love of Christ? Will hardship, or distress, or persecution, or famine, or nakedness, or peril, or sword? ...

No, in all these things we are more than conquerors through him who loved us. For I am convinced that neither death, nor life, nor angels, nor rulers, nor things present, nor things to come, nor powers, nor height, nor depth, nor anything else in all creation, will be able to separate us from the love of God in Christ Jesus our Lord.

Out of Scotland comes a story about a man who lived there many years ago. His name was Joseph Craik. He became known all over Scotland as "the man who turns inkblots into angels." Joseph Craik was a talented and creative penman who could write and draw beautifully. He was appointed as writing master in a village school in Scotland. Often, as children will do when they are learning, his young pupils would leave inkblots on their pages.

While most teachers would chastise the students, circling the inkblots in graphic red and taking away points for sloppy penmanship, Joseph Craik would do something quite different and delightful. Taking his talented pen in hand, and beginning with the blots made by the children, he would add a line here and another one there, and out of the inkblots would come pictures of angels!

So when the students were given back their papers, they weren't all marked up with harsh criticisms. Rather, they were wonderfully decorated with exquisite angels! The children were delighted and pleased and encouraged. And Joseph Craik became a legend in his own time, known far and wide as the man who turned inkblots into angels!

This is a great parable for the Christian faith. By the miracle of his grace, God can take the inkblots of our lives and turn them into angels. God can take our feeble efforts and use them for good. God can take our mistakes and redeem them. God can take our burdens and lighten them. God can take our heartaches and heal them.

This is what the Apostle Paul is saying in Romans 8. By the way, this magnificent passage of Scripture is often read at funerals and memorial services. Look again at these powerful words:

> We know that all things work together for good for those who love God, who are called according to his purpose.... What then are we to say about these things? If God is for us, who is against us?... Who will separate us from the love of Christ? Will hardship, or distress, or persecution, or famine, or nakedness, or peril, or sword?... No, in all these things we are more than conquerors through him who loved us. For I am convinced that neither death, nor life, nor angels, nor rulers, nor things present, nor things to come, nor powers, nor height, nor depth, nor anything else in all creation, will be able to separate us from the love of God in Christ Jesus our Lord.

These words are made all the more meaningful because Paul said them. For you see, in his lifetime, the Apostle Paul knew all about hardships and problems and burdens; he knew all about disappointments and heartaches. He knew first-hand the emotional pain of rejection and the physical pain of harsh persecution. He had been criticized and jailed, threatened and run out of town; he had been falsely accused and beaten within an inch of his life. But he never wavered, he never lost faith, because he knew God was with him and that God can redeem any situation, that God can turn inkblots into angels.

For example, when Paul first became a Christian, many of the early Christians in Jerusalem were afraid of him. Others were suspicious, others doubted him. And why not? After all, he had just recently been persecuting Christians. So they rejected him, they pushed him out. Don't you know that hurt Paul? He had been converted. He wanted to help. He wanted to be in the inner circle of the church, but they wouldn't let him in.

But look what God did with that situation—God turned an inkblot into an angel! Since Paul couldn't get in with the Jewish Christians in Jerusalem, he became the great missionary to the Gentiles. He took the gospel to new places and new people, dramatically reminding the church that Jesus Christ came for *all* people. Don't you wonder what would have happened if that inkblot had not come into Paul's life? If that inkblot had not come, what would have happened to the church—and to the world? That's something to think about, isn't it?

If Paul had been accepted into the Jewish Christian community in Jerusalem with open arms, he might never have gone to Ephesus, to Galatia, to Corinth, to Philippi, or to all those other places he touched with the message of Christ.

But another blow fell on Paul. He wanted so much to go to Spain, the outermost region of the known world at the time. But he never got there! Instead, he went to prison in Rome. Now, Paul could have resented that. He could have cursed the darkness and cried out, "After all I've done, why did God let this happen to me?" Or he could have accepted it stoically, given up, and said, "Oh well I've done my part. Let somebody else worry about it now."

But no, look what happened. Again, God turned that inkblot into an angel. For there in his prison cell, Paul took that opportunity to write, and what he wrote became sacred pages of holy Scripture. There in his prison cell, he wrote much of what we now call the New Testament. After twenty years of nonstop missionary wanderings, Paul had time on his hands and God by his side. He had time to think and meditate and penetrate the deep mysteries of Christ and the Christian faith— and time to write it all down!

Well, the point is clear: It is one of the greatest promises in the whole Bible. God can take bad things and turn them into good things. He can take inkblots and turn them into angels! Let me show you how this amazing promise can work in our lives.

God Can Turn Our Despair into Hope

God can take the inkblot of despair and, with a line here and there, turn it into an angel of hope.

Have you heard about the tour guide who was noted for embellishing the truth? He was somewhat like the preacher, whose son said, "Dad doesn't lie; he just remembers big!"

This tour guide was indeed "remembering big" one day as he led his group through a dark and primitive corner of Africa noted for its dangerous animals. As they walked through the dense jungle, the tour guide showed them a place where he once had to outrun an angry tiger. He then showed them a place where he once had to outswim a hungry crocodile, and another place where he once had to outwit a charging rhino. Finally, he showed them a place where he once had to escape from a ferocious lion.

"How did you get away from that lion?" they asked.

The guide looked straight up and pointed to a limb some twenty feet above his head.

"Don't tell us you jumped way up there to grab that limb," they said.

To which the guide replied, "I missed it going up, but I caught it coming down!"

That happens to us spiritually so often. We miss God on the way up. We're so busy trying to get ahead, to make it to the top, that we miss God—but God is there to catch us on the way down. You know, at first glance, it seems that it ought to be the other way around—that we would be most aware of and tuned in to God when everything is beautiful, when we are on the way up, and all the breaks are going our way. But, the truth is that God is never closer to us than when we are hurting, when we are coming down, filled with despair.

I've often heard people say something like this: "This is the worst thing that's ever happened to us, but we are going to make it through because God is with us. We can feel God's presence as never before." I think there are a couple of reasons for that. For one thing, God is like a loving parent, and we know how loving parents want to be with their children when they are hurting. Also, when we are down-and-out, we are more open to God; we are more willing to cry out for God.

The noted writer Frederick Buechner tells about a low point in his life when God broke through in an unusual way. Buechner was terribly depressed, frightened and worried about his daughter, who was critically ill. He was weighted down with despair and needed a word of assurance from God. Then one day as he sat in his car by the roadside, worried sick about his daughter, a car passed, seeming to come from nowhere—and he got his word from God.

The car had one of those personalized license plates, and it bore on it one word—the one word out of the whole dictionary that Frederick Buechner needed most to see at exactly that moment. The word was TRUST. God's message was revealed on the license plate of a passing car! For Frederick Buechner, it was one of those life-transforming moments that cannot be explained. The burden he had felt was lifted. He did trust God again, he did feel the power of hope filling his heart, and he was renewed, strengthened, reborn.

Who was the owner of the mysterious car with the license plate that said TRUST? Was it a theologian, trying to communicate hope to a desperate world? Was it a minister, giving a one-word sermon? Well, actually, it was the trust officer at the local bank! And this reminds us once again that God works in strange and wondrous ways.

Later, the trust officer gave that license plate to Frederick Buechner, who placed it on a bookshelf in his home, where, to this moment, it serves to remind him daily to trust in God.

"It is rusty around the edges and a little battered," he says, "and it is also as holy a relic as I have ever seen."
(Adapted from Frederick Buechner, *Telling Secrets* [New York: HarperCollins, 1991], pp. 49-50.)

God can turn an inkblot of despair into an angel of hope. And that's not all God can do for us.

God Can Turn Our Problems into Opportunities

There is an urban legend that has been making the rounds about a famous businessman. It says that during the California Gold Rush, a young man from Bavaria came to San Francisco, bringing with him some rolls of canvas. He was twenty years old at the time, and he planned to sell the canvas to the gold miners to use for tents. Then the profits from his sales would finance his own diggings for gold. However, as he headed toward the Sierra Mountains, he met one of the gold miners. When he told the miner his plan, the miner said, "It won't work. It's a waste of your time. Nobody will buy your canvas for tents. That's not what we need."

"O Lord, help me," the young man prayed within. "I've come all this way, and they don't need my canvas for tents. O Lord, what in the world am I going to do?" Then he got his answer.

The gold miner went on: "You should have brought pants. That's what we need—durable pants! Pants don't wear worth a hoot up there in the diggin's. Can't get a pair strong enough." Right then, the young man from Bavaria decided to turn the rolls of canvas into pants—blue pants, that would survive the rigors of the gold-mining camps. He had a harness maker reinforce the pockets with copper studs, and the pants sold like hot cakes! By the way, the name of the young man from Bavaria was Levi Strauss. And he called the new pants "Levi's"! So far, about 900 million pair of Levi's have been sold throughout the world, and they are one of the few items of wearing apparel whose style has remained basically unchanged for more than 130 years.

The point of the story is that God can turn our despair into hope and our problems into opportunities. And ...

God Can Turn Our Defeats into Victories

One of the most significant breakthroughs in medical history occurred in 1967, when a South African physician, Dr. Christiaan Barnard, performed the first successful human heart transplant. In telling about his experiences later, Dr. Barnard said that very often, one of the first requests of a patient was to see the old heart. Dr. Barnard would comply with the request by putting the heart in a jar for the patient to see, and often the patient would say, "Thank you, doctor, for taking away my old diseased heart and giving me a new one."

On a deeper level, that is precisely what God can do for you and me. God can take away our old diseased and defeated heart and give us a new one. That's why we in the church talk so much about new life, new birth, or being born again. Let me ask you—do you need a new heart spiritually? Do you feel down-and-out, defeated? The Great Physician can give you a new heart—and a new start. God can turn your despair into hope, your problems into opportunities, your defeats into victories. In other words—what a promise!—by the miracle of grace, God can turn your inkblots into angels!

7

The Promise of the Holy Spirit

Say Yes to Life

ACTS 2:1-4

When the day of Pentecost had come, they were all together in one place. And suddenly from heaven there came a sound like the rush of a violent wind, and it filled the entire house where they were sitting. Divided tongues, as of fire, appeared among them, and a tongue rested on each of them. All of them were filled with the Holy Spirit and began to speak in other languages, as the Spirit gave them ability.

In *Healing Grace,* Dr. David Seamands tells a story about a farmer who had fallen on hard times. He had gone through several tough years in a row, and his crop production was way down. Consequently, he was having financial problems, so he went to see the manager of his bank.

"I've got some good news and some bad news," he told the banker. "Which would you like to hear first?"

"Let's get the bad news over with first," the banker replied.

"Okay," said the farmer, "what with the bad drought and inflation and all, I won't be able to pay anything on my mortgage this year."

"Well, that's pretty bad," the banker observed.

"Hold on, it gets worse," said the farmer. "I also won't be able to pay anything on the big loan for all that machinery I bought."

"My oh my, things really are bad," the banker exclaimed.

"Well, it's worse than that," the farmer continued. "You remember I also borrowed money to buy seed and fertilizer and other supplies. So of course, I can't pay that back, either."

"That's just awful," the banker said, "but now tell me quickly. What is the good news?"

"The good news," said the farmer, "is that I fully intend to keep doing business with you!"

Now, there's some valuable theology in that story, if we reverse the subjects. The good news of the gospel is that, in spite of our moral bankruptcy, God keeps on doing business with us. That is one of the great promises of the Bible, and in a sense, this is what the Pentecost story in Acts 2 is about. The disciples were spiritually bankrupt: their minds were confused; their confidence was shaken; their nerves were jangled; their strength was sapped; their energy was depleted; their hearts were empty.

Over the preceding few weeks, they had been on an unbelievably emotional roller coaster, with its incredible ups and downs. Just think of it—there was the triumphal entry into Jerusalem on Palm Sunday (that was exhilarating and glorious). But that was quickly followed by the arrest of Jesus; then the trial and the conviction. (They had not counted on that. It wasn't in their game plan. It shook them. It scared the life out of them.)

As if that weren't enough, next came Good Friday and the crucifixion. (That was the toughest blow of all. Their hopes were dashed, their dreams destroyed, their spirits crushed.) But then came Easter morning! (Their Lord was resurrected, and their spirits were resurrected, too. They were ready now to take on the world.)

But then came another jolt! Jesus told them: "I can't stay with you. I must go to my Father, and I want you to take up this torch. I want you to take up this ministry of love! I want you to do it now! I want you to be the church! I want you to teach the world this message of love and sacrifice and commitment and grace. I want you to be my witnesses to all the world."

"But, Lord," they protested, "we can't do that! We don't have the strength. We don't have the know-how. We don't have the power. We don't have the courage."

"Don't worry," the Master promised them. "I won't leave you alone. I will send you a helper. I will send you strength and power. I will send the Holy Spirit to be with you always."

And then Jesus ascended into heaven. And the disciples (per his instructions) waited for the gift of the Holy Spirit. Like little children, they went back to the security of the upper room to think all this through, to sort it out, and to wait for the Holy Spirit. Now, picture this in your mind. Their Lord has gone. The task is squarely on their shoulders. They feel inadequate and frightened. And now they must sit and wait for this Holy Spirit to come.

We know they were never very good at waiting. On earlier occasions when Jesus told them to wait, they either, in their impatience, did the wrong thing, or in their apathy, fell asleep. Now, here they are, waiting, and I can just imagine their grumbling and griping: "This waiting is driving me up the wall. How long do we have to hang around here, anyway?" "We don't know anything about this Holy Spirit. I've never seen any Holy Spirit. I mean, how do we know it really exists?" "Maybe we misunderstood him. We've been here a long time, and nothing has happened. Maybe no Holy Spirit is coming." "Maybe it's over—maybe we should just face that and accept it, just give up and go back to our old lives."

"No!" says Simon Peter. "We wait! He promised us the Holy Spirit will come, and I believe him with all my heart. I believe him!" And just at that moment, they heard something—a strange sound, away off in the distance, becoming louder and louder as it moved toward them, a sound like the rush of a mighty wind—and it blew on that place! (Oh my, did it blow on that place!) And they were all filled with the Holy Spirit.

And they received courage and confidence and strength and new life. Through the power and presence of the Holy Spirit, they said Yes to life, and they became the church of the living God on that day of Pentecost. Through the gift of the Holy Spirit, they were empowered to take up the preaching, teaching, healing, caring ministry of Jesus Christ.

Have you heard the story about the young man who approached the father of his girlfriend to ask his permission for them to marry? The father was skeptical.

He said, "Son, I like you. I think you are a fine person, but I honestly don't think you know what you're asking for. My daughter has very extravagant tastes. I doubt very much that you will ever be able to support her. I'm a wealthy man, and I can barely manage it myself."

The young man thought for a moment before he answered: "Sir, I think I have it. You and I could just pool our resources!"

That's the promise of Pentecost, isn't it? We are not alone! God is with us! We can pool our resources with God, and God's strength will see us through—it will carry us; it will save us. Because of Pentecost, because of the gift of the Holy Spirit, because of God's sustaining presence with us, as Christian people, we can face the future with steady eyes and hopeful hearts.

Even when things sometimes look bleak and dreary and scary, we can live with courage and confidence and grace, because God is with us. Let me show you what I mean.

First, the Holy Spirit Enables Us to Say Yes to Life

In those critical days after the crucifixion, I imagine that there were some hard, uncertain, discouraging moments, when the disciples were tempted to throw in the towel and quit on life. We all know the feeling.

The Reverend Roland Rolheiser, O.M.I., is a teacher at Newman Theological College in Alberta, Canada. He also writes for *The Catholic Herald* in London. A few years ago, he wrote an article called "Ten Commandments for the Long Haul"—Ten Commandments for facing life over a long period. Let me share them with you:

1. Be grateful: Never look a gift universe in the mouth.

2. Don't be naive about God. He will not settle for less than everything.

3. Walk forward when possible. When it feels impossible, try putting one foot in front of the other.

4. Pray that God will hang onto you.

5. Love. Put love first in your life. If a life is large enough for love, it is large enough.

6. Accept what you are—and don't be afraid to be who you are.

7. Refuse to take yourself too seriously; laugh at yourself regularly.

8. Don't be afraid to be softhearted. Redemption lies in tears.

9. Stay with the folks. Remember—you are on a group outing.

10. Don't mummify. Stay alive and alert, and celebrate life.

(Roland Rolheiser, *Celebration*, July 1990.)

When I first discovered Rolheiser's list, I found all of them helpful and thought provoking, but the one that caught my attention most was that last one—"Don't mummify." In other words, "Don't quit on life and walk through your days like a mummy." By the way, Webster defines *mummy* as "lifeless flesh." If you've ever seen a mummy, you know that there is something physical there—there's a body there, but it is lifeless! There is no breath, no heartbeat, no vitality, no spirit, no soul, no life.

Sadly, some living people are like that. They have become disillusioned with life. They have lost their fire, their drive, their hope. Somberly, they just go through the motions. They get up in the morning, they go to work, they eat, they sleep, they exist, they endure, they watch TV. But they are "mummified"! They have thrown in the towel. They have given up. They have quit on life. They have no zest, no joy, no spirit. They are "lifeless" flesh. They are all wrapped up in the clothes of death and defeat. They have forgotten how to seize the moment and celebrate life. So they trudge, they drift, they stonewall, they tune out, they "mummify." Please don't let that happen to you. Please don't drop out. God has a better plan for us than that. God has a better way. Let me give you an example.

Some years ago, a fire broke out in a hotel in Chicago. Flames and smoke blocked the normal escape routes. Some people on the tenth floor went out on a balcony to escape the smoke, but they were trapped there. It looked as if they were doomed. However, one man in the group braved the smoke and went back into the building. Fortunately, he found an exit to a fire escape. He made his way back through the smoke and flames and led the group to safety.

Another person in the group said later, "You can't imagine the feeling of relief and joy we felt when that man came back for us and said, 'This way out. Follow me. I know the way.'" This is what the Christian gospel says to us: "Here is One who knows the way to safety and life. Here is One who can deliver you. Here is One who can save you. Follow him, and you can live!"

Now, there is a sad footnote to that story about the Chicago hotel fire that serves as a parable for us. When the man came back to save the people, some of them followed his lead—but some refused to go with him. They didn't believe him, they didn't trust him, they didn't follow him. They gave up, they mummified, they stayed on the balcony—and eventually they died. Life was there for them, but they refused to accept it, and they perished.

Please don't let that happen to you. Say Yes to the Savior. Say Yes to the Holy Spirit, and the Holy Spirit will enable you to say Yes to life!

Second, the Holy Spirit Enables Us to Say Yes to Other People

On the day of Pentecost, people from many different nations were brought together, and the Holy Spirit enabled them to communicate, to understand one another. The Holy Spirit brought them together.

When the noted poet Edwin Markham reached the age of retirement, he discovered that his banker had stolen much of his retirement money. He was heartsick. Understandably, he felt hurt and betrayed, and he became bitter. As the days passed, his bitterness became such a poisonous venom within him that he could no longer write poetry. He could only entertain thoughts of revenge.

One day while sitting at his desk, thinking about the man who had so wronged him, he suddenly felt the Spirit of God sweeping over him, saying, "Markham, if you do not deal with this thing, it's going to ruin you. You cannot afford the price you are paying. You must forgive that man."

Following the lead of the Holy Spirit, Edwin Markham dropped to his knees and prayed: "Lord, I will, and I do freely forgive that man." Later he said, "Then a miracle occurred. The resentment was gone and the poetry began to flow once again." In fact, soon after that, Edwin Markham sat down and wrote his most famous poem, "Outwitted":

> He drew a circle that shut me out—
> Heretic, rebel, a thing to flout.
> But Love and I had the wit to win:
> We drew a circle that took him in!

It is the powerful presence of the Holy Spirit that enables us to forgive like that, to love like that. The Holy Spirit enables us to say Yes to life, and to say Yes to other people.

Third, the Holy Spirit Enables Us to Say Yes to God

We can say Yes to God because God has already said Yes to us.

If we were to make a list of the most beloved hymns of all time, one certain to make the list would be the gospel hymn "Just As I Am." It has been called the world's greatest soul-winning hymn, partly due to the influence of Billy Graham and his crusades. As a young man, Billy Graham walked to the altar in his conversion to the singing of that hymn, and ever since, his crusades on every continent have used it as the invitation hymn.

But the real power of that hymn is found in the one who wrote the words many years ago. Her name was Charlotte Elliott. She was born in England in 1789. When she was thirty-two, she suffered a rare illness that left her a permanent invalid. She sank into great despair and into angry, hostile rebellion against God. The next year, her concerned father brought a minister into their home to talk with his daughter. God was with that minister that day. He said just the right words in just the right tone of voice, and suddenly the presence of God was felt powerfully in that room.

When Charlotte Elliott felt the Holy Spirit touching her heart, she gave up her rebellion, placed her complete trust in Jesus Christ, and accepted him as her Savior. From that moment until her death at age eighty-two, she always celebrated her birthday on that date—the day of her spiritual birth.

"That's the day I really came alive," she said. "The day I accepted Christ as my Lord and Savior is my real birthday." Later, she wrote the famous hymn that is her own spiritual autobiography:

> Just as I am, without one plea,
> but that thy blood was shed for me,
> and that thou bidst me come to thee,
> O Lamb of God, I come, I come.

It's the Holy Spirit that enables us to say Yes to life, Yes to other people, and Yes to God.

8

The Promise of Hope

The Light Shines, and the Darkness Cannot Overcome It

JOHN 1:1-5

In the beginning was the Word, and the Word was with God, and the Word was God. He was in the beginning with God. All things came into being through him, and without him not one thing came into being. What has come into being in him was life, and the life was the light of all people. The light shines in the darkness, and the darkness did not overcome it.

Her name is Nancy Kerrigan. She was a world-class athlete. The twenty-four-year-old ice-skater from a middle-class Boston suburb wanted very badly to win her second national crown before the 1994 Winter Olympics in Lillehammer, Norway. This had been her dream since she was six years old. Over the years, her father had worked two, sometimes three, jobs to keep her in skates and pay for her training. And for the last eighteen years, he had arisen every morning at 4:30 to drive his daughter to the ice rink for her practice.

Nancy Kerrigan's mother lost her eyesight to a virus when Nancy was just a baby. She had to press her face to a TV monitor so that she could see the shadows as her daughter performed on the ice.

"I never see her hand. I never see her face," said Mrs. Kerrigan. "I would do anything to see her. There are times when I say, 'Come here, Nancy. I just want to look at you.' We sit nose-to-nose and I try to see what everyone else sees in her." What America saw in Nancy Kerrigan was one of the most accomplished and graceful U.S. figure skaters, our brightest and best Olympic hopeful.

But then a shocking, stunning nightmare! Nancy had just finished a practice session for the national championships in Detroit, when suddenly a man approached. Without warning, he delivered a violent blow to her right leg with a clublike object. Nancy Kerrigan went down in pain, screaming and crying. Her father ran to her, scooped her up in his arms, and rushed her to a nearby hospital. She was treated and released, but was injured seriously enough to force her to withdraw from the competition—an event she had been favored to win. Although unable to compete in the nationals, she was selected for the Olympic team.

In the days after the attack, the plot thickened. It became known that the brutal attack had been performed by a "hit man" hired by supporters of another figure skater. Nancy Kerrigan later said, "When I went down, I cried, 'Why me?' But the right question isn't 'why me'? It's why anybody?"

When I heard what had happened in Detroit, my mind immediately darted back to what had happened to Monica Seles in Hamburg, just nine months before. She was the number-one woman tennis player in the world at the time. Unbelievably, she was stabbed in the back on a tennis court—the victim of an unemployed German lathe operator who wanted to injure her so that his favorite, Steffi Graf, could become number one.

That happened in April of 1993, and arguably, Monica Seles's career never fully recovered. But she did reach out to comfort, console, and encourage Nancy Kerrigan. Monica Seles said later:

Nancy is an ice skater. I'm a tennis player. Crimes against us are no more tragic than what happens to too many innocent victims every day.... My hope is that this kind of terrible incident will cause us to ... stop senseless violence against innocent victims. (*Newsweek*, Jan. 17, 1994, p. 44)

With that quote about "senseless violence against innocent victims" ringing in my ears, I reached over and picked up the morning newspaper to see how many articles in one day's paper would describe that kind of brutal activity. In that one newspaper, there were 3 articles about murders, 4 about cruel muggings and robberies, 2 about street gangs, 1 about youth vandalism, 2 about child abuse, 2 about drug dealers, 3 about threats of war, 1 about nuclear missiles, and 2 about hate groups.

What is happening to us? What in the world is going on? Why is there so much violence today? Some blame it on the breakdown of the family. And it is true that a huge percentage of people involved in criminal activity today do indeed come from broken homes. A few years ago, according to the FBI, over 70 percent of juvenile offenders came from broken homes.

Some point the finger at the media. The average child has watched 8,000 televised murders and 100,000 acts of violence before finishing elementary school. And that doesn't even count the movies. Others blame it on drugs; others on the morally permissive society in which we live; still others point to the easy availability of guns as the culprit. Here are a couple of statistics: One out of every six young people between the ages of 10 and 17 has either seen or knows someone who has been shot. And young people under the age of 18 are 244 percent more likely to be injured or killed by guns today than in 1986.

Well, the point is this: There is a lot of darkness in our world these days. Sometimes we feel almost overwhelmed by the darkness. But you know, despite all the dark shadows that sometimes cover us like a heavy blanket, I am not pessimistic about our present or our future. I am optimistic because I am a Christian. I know about the darkness in our world today. However, I am optimistic because I believe in "the light of the world." Remember how this reads in the first verses of John's Gospel: "The light shines in the darkness, and the darkness did not overcome it." That is the promise of the Scriptures.

Our hope is in Jesus Christ. Ultimately, the victory will be his. He is the light of the world, and the darkness of the world doesn't have a chance against him. Those who believe in peace have written these words:

> At the heart of [any new movement] toward peace will be Jesus the Christ. His way of love is infinitely more powerful than the way of war and violence.... "Darkness cannot drive out darkness; only light can do that. Hate cannot drive out hate; only love can do that."...Jesus Christ attacks evil in its breeding place—the heart of humanity: the hearts of nations, the hearts of institutions, the hearts of persons.... Thousands of years of human experience have proved over and over again that the heart of all transformation is the transformation of the heart. (*Seeking God's Peace in a Nuclear Age*, ed. Ronald Osborn [St. Louis: Chalice Press, 1985], p. 86. Portion within quotation marks is from writings of Martin Luther King, Jr. as cited in Alan Geyer, *The Idea of Disarmament*, p. 216.)

When the noted writer Robert Louis Stevenson was a little boy, he was sitting one night by a window in his room, watching a lamplighter light the streetlights below. When his nurse came in and asked him what he was doing, young Robert answered, "I'm watching a man make holes in the darkness." Every time we lift up Jesus Christ, every time we stand tall for Jesus Christ, every time we live in the spirit of Christ or share the truth of Christ with others, we are punching holes in the darkness! Remember that old Chinese proverb: "It's better to light a candle than to curse the darkness." Indeed so. Two thousand years ago, God lighted the candle and sent it into the world. It is our part to walk in that light, and live in that light, and share that light with our world.

Now let's bring this great promise closer to home by underscoring three significant thoughts that emerge out of this powerful verse in John 1.

First, the Light Overcomes the Darkness of Ignorance

A minister friend of mine once said something that impressed me: "Imagine that you accidentally walk into a dark alley late one night, and suddenly you see ten young men walking briskly toward you. Would it affect how you might feel at that moment, if you knew that those ten young men were coming from a Bible study group?"

It surely would affect how we might feel, because the Bible is a "lamp to our feet." It teaches us to be kind, loving, honest, gracious people. It has within its pages the great truths of God and the great keys for healthy, wholesome living. Take, for example, the Ten Commandments. We can't break them. They are unbreakable, invincible. When we disobey them, we are the ones who get broken! They are our spiritual and moral roots. They are the unshakable, unchanging spiritual laws of God, and they are just as dependable as the law of gravity.

The Ten Commandments are a lamp for us because they tell us how things are—how things hold together, how things work best—and they are as valid for us today as they were for Moses and the people of Israel—indeed, for all the people who have lived or ever will live on the face of this earth.

Frederick Buechner, in *Wishful Thinking*, put it like this: "God's law ... has been stated in eight words. 'He who does not love remains in death' (1 John 3:14). Like it or not, that's how it is. If you don't believe it, you can always put it to the test just the way if you don't believe the law of gravity, you can always step out a tenth-story window" (pp. 50-51).

In her novel *Country of the Pointed Firs,* Sarah Orne Jewett tells about a woman, a writer, who goes to visit Elijah Tilley, a retired sea captain. As she walks up the pathway leading to the main house, she sees something unusual—a number of wooden posts scattered about the property, in no discernible order. Each post was painted white and trimmed in yellow to match the captain's house. When the woman asked the captain about the posts, he explained that when he first plowed the ground, he kept snagging and breaking his plow on the many large rocks hidden just beneath the surface. He said he had set the posts in those particular spots to mark the dangerous rocks in order to avoid them in the future.

In a sense, this is what God has done for us with the Ten Commandments. He has said, "Look! These are the trouble spots in life. Avoid these, and you won't snag your plow." The light of God overcomes the darkness of ignorance.

Second, the Light Overcomes the Darkness of Prejudice

A few years ago, when President George H. W. Bush went to visit a nursing home, he met an elderly gentleman walking down the hall. He went to the man, shook his hand warmly, and then, in a gracious and kindly tone, President Bush asked, "Sir, do you know who I am?"

The man replied, "No, but if you ask the nurses, they can tell you!"

The point is that we don't really know people until we know them well, until we walk in their shoes. That's the problem with prejudice. It literally means "to prejudge," and it causes all kinds of heartache and pain. But again the light of God helps us. It shows us how to reach out to others with love and respect. If every person would live in the gracious spirit of Christ, we could have heaven on earth.

Fred Craddock tells about a missionary named Oswald Golter. Back in the 1940s, his mission board sent him the money to come home from North China after ten years of service there. When he docked at a port in India to await passage home, he found a boatload of refugees housed in a warehouse on the pier. The refugees weren't wanted in many ports, so they were stranded there. It was Christmastime, so the missionary went to the warehouse to visit these refugees.

He said to them, "Merry Christmas! What do you want for Christmas?"

"We're not Christians," they said. "We don't believe in Christmas."

"I know," said the missionary, "but what do you want for Christmas?" They finally mentioned some wonderful German pastries they were fond of, and Oswald Golter scoured the city until he found a bakery that made those pastries. He cashed in his ticket home, bought baskets and baskets of the pastries, took them to the refugees, and wished them a merry Christmas.

When he later told the story, a student said, "But sir, why did you do that for them? They weren't Christians. They don't even believe in Jesus."

"I know," he replied, "but I do!"
(Fred Craddock, *Newscope Inspiration Series* tape, Jan. 1990.)

The Light of Christ overcomes the darkness of ignorance and the darkness of prejudice.

Third, the Light Overcomes the Darkness of Sin

Dr. Edgar Dewitt Jones tells about preaching a revival one time. When he gave the invitation, a huge, burly man came storming down the aisle. He was obviously moved, penitent and remorseful. Big tears were streaming down his cheeks.

He marched right to the front, stuck out his hand to Dr. Jones, and said, "Preacher, you said tonight that God could save anybody, no matter who they are or what they've done. I want to believe that. I want him to save me. But I want you to know I've done everything. I've done it all. So many times, I've broken the Ten Commandments—all of them. I'm a Swedish blacksmith by trade, and I have been a terrible sinner. I don't know whether God can help me or not."

Dr. Jones took his massive hand, looked deep into that eager face, and said to him, "Sir, you are in luck. God is specializing in Swedish blacksmiths tonight!"

(Thanks to Buckner Fanning, Trinity Baptist Church, San Antonio)

I don't know what your sin is. Maybe it's something so overt and so obvious that everyone around you knows about it. Or maybe it's some secret sin. But whatever it is, God is specializing in you today. God is the Great Physician, and God can bring healing where it hurts. The Good Shepherd wants to welcome you into the flock. God is the Light of the World, and that light can overcome any darkness. We have to do our part—we have to accept God into our hearts. We have to come to God in faith and trust and penitence and commitment. And when we do, God will welcome us with open arms and light up our lives. That's a promise of hope that we can stand on with confidence!

9

The Promise of Resurrection

When Easter Calls Your Name

JOHN 20:11-18

But Mary stood weeping outside the tomb. As she wept, she bent over to look into the tomb; and she saw two angels in white, sitting where the body of Jesus had been lying, one at the head and the other at the feet. They said to her, "Woman, why are you weeping?" She said to them, "They have taken away my Lord, and I do not know where they have laid him."

When she had said this, she turned around and saw Jesus standing there, but she did not know it was Jesus. Jesus said to her, "Woman, why are you weeping? Whom are you looking for?" Supposing him to be the gardener, she said to him, "Sir, if you have carried him away, tell me where you have laid him, and I will take him away." Jesus said to her, "Mary!" She turned and said to him in Hebrew, "Rabbouni!" (which means Teacher).

Jesus said to her, "Do not hold on to me, because I have not yet ascended to the Father. But go to my brothers and say to them, 'I am ascending to my Father and your Father, to my God and your God.' " Mary Magdalene went and announced to the disciples, *"I have seen the Lord"; and she told them that he had said these things to her.*

Bill Bryson has written a fascinating book called *The Lost Continent: Travels in Small Town America.* In one chapter, he tells of traveling to Hannibal, Missouri, to visit the boyhood home of the noted author Mark Twain. He described the house as a "tidy whitewashed house with green shutters set incongruously in the middle of downtown." It costs $2.00 to visit Mark Twain's home and walk around the site.

Bryson said he found the home to be a disappointment: "It purported to be a faithful reproduction of the original interiors, but there were wires and water sprinklers clumsily evident in every room. I also very much doubt that young Samuel Clemens's bedroom had Armstrong vinyl on the floor . . . or that his sister's bedroom had a plywood partition in it." The house is owned by the city of Hannibal and attracts some 135,000 visitors each year.

Bryson was also disappointed that he was not able to actually go inside the house. "You look through the windows," he says. "At each window there is a recorded message telling you about that room."

As he proceeded from window to window, he met another tourist who seemed to know a lot about the house. Bryson asked him, "What do you think of it?"

The friendly stranger replied, "Oh, I think it's great. I always come here whenever I'm in Hannibal—two, three times a year. Sometimes I go out of my way to come here."

Bill Bryson was fascinated. "Really?" he exclaimed.

"Oh yes," the man went on, "I must have been here twenty or thirty times by now. This is a real shrine, you know."

As they continued walking and touring, Bill Bryson commented, "You must be a real fan and follower of

Mark Twain. Would you say the house is just like Mark Twain described it in his books?"

"I don't know," answered the tourist. "Wouldn't have the foggiest notion. I've never read any of his books!"

(Thanks to Rod Wilmoth, St. Paul United Methodist Church, Omaha, Nebraska, for this illustration in his sermon on 1-17-93.)

Visiting his shrine, but ignoring his books. Sadly, that may be a pretty good description of the way many people deal with Jesus Christ. They visit his shrines, but fail to accept him or follow him, or apply his teachings to their daily lives.

As a matter of fact, I had a similar experience at the Garden Tomb in Jerusalem some years ago, with a Holy Land tour group. One morning we came to the Garden Tomb, the site of the resurrection.

I can't find the words to express the thrill of that experience, the exhilaration of being in that sacred place. We walked around that beautiful garden. We went inside that empty tomb. We touched the massive stone that had been rolled away from the door of the grave. We stood together in that holy place and celebrated Holy Communion. We prayed there for loved ones. And we sang "Christ the Lord Is Risen Today." It was an incredible moment, a powerfully spiritual moment for me.

After that, people in the group began taking pictures. I noticed a man sitting on a bench nearby. He had been watching us. I walked over and sat down beside him.

"I just love this place," he said. "It's so serene and quiet here. I come here two or three times a week to enjoy this."

"You must be a devoted Christian," I said to him.

"Oh, no!" he protested. "I'm not a Christian at all. I just think it's real pretty here."

This is always the temptation we face in our faith pilgrimage, isn't it?—to visit the shrine, enjoy the beauty, and yet not really personally experience the Risen Lord.

It is important to notice that Easter did not become real for Mary until it became personal, until Easter called her by name. When the Risen Christ said, "Mary," when it became a personal experience for her, then it became real, powerful, authentic, life-changing. And at that moment, Mary was resurrected, too! She too received new life!

Remember the story with me. On the Thursday night before Easter, Jesus was arrested on trumped-up charges. He was brutally beaten, rushed through a fixed trial held strangely in the middle of the night, and declared guilty. The next day, Good Friday, Jesus was crucified and buried in a borrowed grave. And then on Easter morning, Mary Magdalene came to the tomb.

The stone that had been covering the opening to the grave had been rolled away. She looked inside. She was startled to see that his body was gone. She thought someone had broken into the grave and stolen it. She was crushed, heartbroken, devastated—"They crucified him, and now they have taken his body away. How could they be so cruel?" she cried.

But then she heard a noise behind her. She turned and saw the silhouette of a man she thought was the gardener—until he called her by name. "Mary," he said tenderly. She recognized that voice, and at that moment she ran headlong into Easter. She realized the truth. It was Christ!

His body had not been stolen. He had risen. He had conquered death. He had defeated evil. He had come back to life. He was resurrected. She had come to the tomb that Easter morning looking for a dead body and found, instead, a Risen Lord!

And with that discovery, Mary too was resurrected! No more weeping and wailing. No more heavy sighing. No more tears of sorrow. He sent her running and shouting the good news: "I have seen the Lord! I have seen the Lord! He is risen!"

On that Easter morning long ago, the key moment came when the Risen Lord called Mary by name. Well, the Risen Lord is still speaking, and he is calling your name and mine. Can you hear him? He is calling us by name. He is telling us that he has conquered death, and he promises that we too can be resurrected with him. He wants to share, with each one of us, the joy, the encouragement, and the forgiveness that come when he resurrects us and gives us new life.

The Risen Lord Wants to Share with Us the Joy of Resurrection

Mary Magdalene came to the tomb filled with despair, but Easter changed all that. It gave her an amazing, indescribable joy. Let me tell you about Philip.

Philip was eight years old, and he attended the third-grade Sunday school class at his church. Philip was a special little boy. He was deeply loved by his family, but sometimes society didn't quite know how to respond to Philip because, you see, he had Down's Syndrome. The other children in the third-grade Sunday school class didn't include him very often. It wasn't that they were mean or cruel. It was just that they were only eight years old, and they didn't understand why Philip was different. They didn't realize how special he was.

However, one Easter Sunday morning, a wonderful thing happened. The teacher came up with a creative plan. She told the children the story of Easter, and then she gave each of them one of those plastic eggs that opens up.

She said to them, "Take your egg, go outside, and find something that reminds you of new life and Easter! Put it in your egg and bring it back, and put it in our Easter basket. Then we will open them for all to see and share." The children were delighted, and they rushed outside.

Soon they were all back and had put all their plastic eggs in the big Easter basket. Then the teacher began to open the eggs.

A little girl in the class had put a flower in her egg, to

show how only God could make a beautiful blossom like that. Another little girl had put a butterfly in her egg. She said she remembered that the butterfly was one of the church's symbols for Easter. A little boy had put a rock in his egg. He explained, "I knew the girls would pick flowers and stuff, so I found a rock to remind us that the stone was rolled away from the tomb."

The teacher was pleased. This was going quite well. But when she opened the fourth egg, it was empty! This upset the students. "Unfair! No fun! Somebody cheated! Somebody didn't do it right!" they complained in frustration.

"It's mine," said Philip.

"Oh, Philip," they said. "You never do anything right!"

"I did so do it right!" Philip argued. "It's empty because the tomb was empty! It's *supposed* to be empty because Christ arose!"

There was a sudden stunned silence in the room—and then the miracle of Easter happened again. The children began to cheer for Philip. They ran to him and hugged him and patted him on the back.

"Way to go, Philip," they said. "You did great!" "You did best of all!" And Philip beamed with joy—the joy of Easter! From that moment, Philip was accepted and respected and included and loved.

That Easter Sunday morning, those children celebrated not only the resurrection of Christ, but the resurrection of young Philip. This is the good news of Easter, the joy of Easter—that Christ came back to life, and he chooses to share his victory with you and me ... and with all the Philips of the world.

The Risen Lord Wants to Share with Us the Encouragement of Resurrection

Bishop Kenneth Goodson loved to tell the story about a famous painting of the crucifixion that was placed on display in a downtown store window in Winston-Salem, North Carolina, during Holy Week one year. He said the depiction of the blood dripping from the crown of thorns was so real, you wanted to reach out and wipe it away.

Early one morning a businessman stopped to look at the painting. He was joined by a newspaper boy making his early deliveries. After a few moments of silence, the man turned to walk away, shaking his head, tears misting his eyes, and muttering to himself, "What a pity! What a shame!"

The newspaper boy heard him, and as the man started across the street, the boy shouted after him: "Hey, Mister! Didn't you know? Haven't you heard? He ain't dead anymore. He's alive! He's alive!"

Sometimes the Good Fridays of the world do indeed make us shake our heads and mutter, "What a pity. What a shame." But then along comes Easter to remind us that there is no evil strong enough to keep Christ in the grave.

He will win! Goodness will win! Truth will win! Love will win! Ultimately, God will win! And through faith in God, the victory can be ours as well. If that doesn't encourage you, I don't know what will. That's the joy of Easter and that's the encouragement of Easter.

The Risen Lord Wants to Share with Us the Forgiveness of Resurrection

On Good Friday, Jesus died on the cross for our sins, and then on Easter morning, he arose to assure us that we are forgiven.

Some of you know that my father died in a car wreck when I was thirteen years old. I read it in the newspaper before anyone could reach me to tell me about it. When I saw that picture of our smashed-up car on the front page of the newspaper, and read that my dad had died in that accident, I was thrust immediately and painfully into the shocked numbness of deep grief.

Strangely, one of my very first thoughts was covered with guilt. I remembered that, some months before at a family picnic, I had been showing off with a baseball. I threw it wildly, and it hit my dad and broke his thumb. I felt so bad about that. What a terrible son I was! I had caused my dad great pain. And I lived with that guilt for several months. Finally, I went to my pastor and admitted these deep feelings of guilt about breaking my dad's thumb.

I'll never forget how my pastor handled that. He was so great. He came around the desk with tears in his eyes.

He sat down across from me and said, "Now, Jim, you listen to me. If your dad could come back to life for five minutes and be right here with us, and if he knew you were worried about that, what would he say to you?"

I answered, "He would tell me to quit worrying about that."

"Well, all right," the pastor said. "Then you quit worrying about that right now. Do you understand me?"

"Yes, sir." I said, and I did. That minister was saying to me, you are forgiven. Accept that forgiveness, and make a new start with your life.

Something like that happened at Easter. The Risen Lord came back to life, and he assured the disciples that they were forgiven. Peter had denied his Lord three times. All the disciples had forsaken him. Thomas still doubted. But Christ came back to forgive them and resurrect them. He came back to share with them—and with us—the joy, the encouragement, and the forgiveness of Easter.

10

The Promise of Happiness

The Roads to Happiness

JOHN **14:1-6**

"Do not let your hearts be troubled. Believe in God, believe also in me. In my Father's house there are many dwelling places. If it were not so, would I have told you that I go to prepare a place for you? And if I go and prepare a place for you, I will come again and will take you to myself, so that where I am, there you may be also. And you know the way to the place where I am going."

Thomas said to him, "Lord, we do not know where you are going. How can we know the way?" Jesus said to him, "I am the way, and the truth, and the life. No one comes to the Father except through me."

Have you heard about the little boy who was trying to raise some money by collecting old bottles, going door-to-door in his neighborhood? When he came to the home of a woman who was the "town grouch," the little boy asked, "Do you have any old soda bottles?"

"No!"

Then he said, "Do you have any old whiskey bottles?"

"Young man," the woman retorted, "Do I look like the type of person who would have old whiskey bottles?"

The little boy studied her for a moment and then asked, "Well, do you have any old vinegar bottles?"

Isn't it tragic that some people go through life so sad, so sour, so bitter, that their unhappiness literally shows on their faces? God meant life to be full, happy, joyous, and meaningful. All the Beatitudes start with that premise:

"Blessed are the merciful ..."

"Blessed are the peacemakers ..."

"Blessed are the pure in heart ..."

The word *blessed* in Matthew 5 literally means, "How happy!" "How radiant!" "How full!"

But the stark fact is that many people never find the road to happiness. They search for it, they long for it, they spend lots of money, time, and effort striving for it. Desperately, they want happiness, but somehow it eludes them, because they look in all the wrong places, they go down all the wrong roads, and they come up empty, the sad picture of disillusionment.

A friend of mine recently shared with me an experience in an art museum in New York. She went into one special exhibit room where all the paintings were of roads. There were paintings of busy modern interstate highways, big city crowded thoroughfares, attractive landscaped parkways, happy neighborhood streets, remote mountain trails, and quiet country roads.

At one end of the big room was a very large painting of a road. It had an ethereal, spiritual look, with soft pastel colors, and the caption beneath it read: "The Road to Happiness." As my friend stood there and looked at this magnificent painting, two fashionably dressed, middle-aged women walked up beside her. One of them was visibly moved by the painting.

"Isn't that beautiful?" she said.

But the other responded sadly, "Of course it's beautiful. The only problem is, there's no such road!"

All of us have had moments like that, haven't we, moments when we could say with that woman in the

New York City art gallery, "There's no such road" to happiness! The great philosopher Henry David Thoreau once suggested that every person we meet is living in "quiet desperation." Evidently, Thoreau had sensed that there are lots of unhappy people in our world. We touch shoulders every day with people who are carrying heavy, private burdens in their hearts, burdens we know nothing about, and many of these people have become sadly convinced that "there's no such road to happiness."

It seems that this always has been humankind's great burden of doubt. Many people feel, "There is no such road for me." But the Christian faith sees it differently. The Christian faith has a road, a path, a way. That is precisely what this classic passage in John 14 is about; it is one of the highest mountain peaks in the whole Bible. Jesus says, "Do not let your hearts be troubled. [Don't be so unhappy.] ... I am the way, and the truth, and the life."

Even though we often read this passage at a time of death (and appropriately so), it is packed with the stuff of life, and the point is clear—Christ is the road to happiness. He shows us the way, he reveals to us the truth, he gives us the life. The key to happiness is not clout out there; it is Christ within! It is not dollars out there; it is discipleship within! It is not possession of material things out there; it is being possessed by the Messiah within! It is not having securities out there; it is having the Savior within. He is the Way, the Truth, and the Life. He is the Road to Happiness. That's a promise!

With that in mind, let's take a look at the biblical roads to happiness. We will find Christ right in the middle of every one of them.

There Is the Road to Damascus (The Road of Conversion)

This is the road where the Risen Christ confronted Saul of Tarsus. Saul was so dramatically changed on that road that he wanted to change his name. He became Paul. Talk about a conversion! There Saul, the persecutor of Christians, became Paul, the missionary for Christ. His direction was changed. His allegiance was changed. His commitment was changed. His life was changed.

Now, let me ask you. Have you been converted like that? Has Christ turned your life around like that? The truly happy, fulfilled people in this world are those who have been forgiven and converted. The genuinely radiant people in this life are those who, by the miracle of God's grace, have been changed from self-centeredness to Christ-centeredness.

Dr. James Simpson, one of the great medical minds of an earlier generation, was a Scottish surgeon who made many important medical breakthroughs, including the use of anesthesia. Toward the end of his life, someone asked him what he considered his greatest discovery. He answered: "The greatest discovery of my life is that I am a great sinner, and Jesus is a great Savior!"

All the other discoveries pale in comparison to this one. This is the discovery of the Damascus Road, what the Christian faith has traditionally called "being converted," "being forgiven," "being set right with God." And I'm convinced that until we find that oneness with God, we can't really find happiness. As Saint Augustine put it, "My soul is restless, O God, 'til it finds its rest in Thee." So the first road to happiness is the Road to Damascus, the road of forgiveness and conversion.

There Is the Road to Jericho (The Road of Kindness)

It's the road the good Samaritan walked, where he reached out in compassion to touch the life of a person in need. That gentle act has lived through the ages as the great classic symbol of Christian kindness and service to others. If you want to be happy, learn how to be kind in the spirit of Christ. Dedicate your life to being the instrument of God's tenderness to others.

In May of 1989, Senator John C. Danforth gave the Commencement address at Rockhurst College. What would he say to these young people who have been preparing for adulthood? His words caught the audience by surprise:

> Members of the Class of 1989, today you celebrate the completion of sixteen years of formal education. You look back on all the important things—the good things you learned in those sixteen years. You do so with a justifiable pride that is shared by your family and teachers who are here with you at this ceremony. I share your joy in those good things you learned, and I congratulate you for them. But I'm not going to dwell on those things this morning. Instead, I want to speak of the bad thing you learned—the Dark Thing. I want to shed some light on the Dark Thing and to challenge you to do something about it.
>
> The Dark Thing you learned is meanness—plain old-fashioned cruelty. All school children learn it. They learn it on the first playground on the first day of first grade. They learn to laugh at the fat kid, the slow kid, the kid who can't catch a ball or do a somersault. It is a cruel laughter and it hurts. It sends some kids home in tears on that first day of school and on many days thereafter. It is the laughter that says, "I'm better than you." It sees our success as dependent upon the defeat of others. Meanness is a temptation to those who are bright, who are achievers. It is a temptation to college graduates.

Well, you can imagine that Senator Danforth caught the attention of his audience. He concluded his speech by quoting a passage from Kurt Vonnegut's *God Bless You, Mr. Rosewater.* Eliot Rosewater had come to baptize the newborn twins of the town outcast, Mary Moody. As he sprinkled water on the twins, he said:

> Hello, babies. Welcome to earth. It's hot in the summer and cold in the winter. It's round and wet and crowded. At the outside, babies, you've got about a hundred years

here. And there's only one rule that I know of, babies—
you've got to be kind!

You've just got to be kind! The second biblical road to
happiness is the Jericho Road—the road of kindness and
service to others.

There Is the Road to Jerusalem (The Road of Faith)

You remember how steadfastly Jesus set his face
toward Jerusalem. He headed there determined to strike a
blow for justice. He knew what awaited him there, but he
walked toward Jerusalem with total confidence and faith.
He knew God would be with him, and he knew God
would bring it out right. This is the road to happiness, the
path of absolute faith, the unflinching confidence that
God's righteousness will ultimately win the day and that
God wants to share that victory with you and me.

I love the story about the two little girls in Sunday
school who were listening as their teacher read the crucifixion story. One of the little girls was jolted by the
details of the story. Suddenly, the horror, the cruelty,
the ugliness of the crucifixion broke through to her
for the first time, and she began to cry.

But her little friend patted her on the arm and said,
"Don't cry, Mary! Don't cry! This is one of God's stories,
and God's stories always turn out good!"

Everything that happens to you and me can be one of
God's stories, and it can "turn out good" if we do our
best and then trust God to finish it. There is great joy and
peace in knowing that road to happiness, the Road to
Jerusalem—the way of faith and trust in God.

There Is the Road to Calvary (The Road of Sacrificial Love)

This is the way of the cross. Have you ever noticed
that when people go out of their way to do something for

others, often the person they have helped will say, "You shouldn't have done that," and invariably they will say, "We were happy to do it." Our world has become confused and distorted; we so often think that happiness is in receiving, but the truth is that the greatest happiness is in giving—sacrificial love.

Some years ago, there was an Archbishop of Paris who was known far and wide for his sacrificial spirit. One Sunday morning, when he was preaching to a great congregation in the famous Notre Dame Cathedral in Paris, he told about an incident that had happened there some years earlier. Three young men, irreverent, selfish, worldly, and godless, wandered into the cathedral one day. Two of them wagered the third that he would not make a bogus confession. The third accepted the bet and went into the confessional.

The priest, who had been listening to the bogus confession, realized what was happening, so when the pretending penitent had finished, the priest said, "To every confession, there is a penance. You see the great crucifix over there? Go to it, kneel down before it, look up into the face of the crucified Lord, and repeat aloud three times, 'All this you did for me, and I don't care at all!'"

The young man emerged laughing from the confessional, to report what had happened and claim the wager from his companions.

"Oh, no," they said. "First complete the penance, and then we will pay the wager."

Walking slowly to the great crucifix, he knelt down and looked up into that face, with its searching eyes of sacrificial love.

Then he began, "All this you did for me, and I ... I ..." He got no further. Tears flooded his eyes. His heart was torn by the pain of repentance. There his old life ended and the new began.

Finishing his sermon, the Archbishop said, "I know that is a true story, because I was that young man."

The spirit of sacrifice—do we know what that means? Have we become too soft? too spoiled? too selfish? Is that why we have trouble finding happiness? The fact is that the truly happy, fulfilled people are those who know how to live in the spirit of Christ, how to live in the spirit of sacrificial love. He is the way, the truth, and the life! He is the road to happiness, and that's a promise on which we can depend, on which we can stand.

11

The Promise of Christlike Living

Do the Teachings of Jesus Still Work?

MATTHEW 5:38-45

"You have heard that it was said, 'An eye for an eye and a tooth for a tooth.' But I say to you, Do not resist an evildoer. But if anyone strikes you on the right cheek, turn the other also; and if anyone wants to sue you and take your coat, give your cloak as well; and if anyone forces you to go one mile, go also the second mile. Give to everyone who begs from you, and do not refuse anyone who wants to borrow from you.

"You have heard that it was said, 'You shall love your neighbor and hate your enemy.' But I say to you, Love your enemies and pray for those who persecute you, so that you may be children of your Father in heaven; for he makes his sun rise on the evil and on the good, and sends rain on the righteous and on the unrighteous."

A few years ago, I was on the campus of a small college during their Religious Emphasis week. The theme of the week was "The Hard Sayings of Jesus"—in other words, the difficult teachings of Jesus. One evening in one of the dormitories, I was leading a discussion on some of these difficult teachings, such as "turn the other cheek," "love your enemies," "go the second mile," and "pray for those who persecute you." One young man said, "The teachings of Jesus are difficult for me because I'm not sure I understand them." Another student said, "I see it just the other way around, just the opposite. They are difficult for me because I think I *do* understand them, but I'm not so sure I want to *do* them."

When you study the Gospels closely, you come face-to-face with the frustrating fact that Jesus did indeed say some very perplexing things. These "difficult sayings" have puzzled many devout Bible readers over the years. Even during his ministry, Jesus' words were often misunderstood by his hearers, and even by his own disciples. There is a vivid example of this in John 6:60, where some of the disciples, after hearing Jesus speak, exclaim, "This is a hard saying; who can listen to it?" *The New English Bible* makes it even more dramatic by translating it this way: "This is more than we can stomach! Why listen to such talk?" Then a few verses later, we find this haunting sentence: "From that time on, many of his disciples withdrew and no longer went about with him" (John 6:66 NEB).

This reveals something very interesting, namely, that the difficulty here is not just in understanding what Jesus meant. In a real sense we could say that when we understand the difficult sayings of Jesus, our difficulty has just begun, because we run head-on into the startling challenges of living the Christian faith. As Jesus saw it, being a Christian disciple meant living in a special kind of sacrificial, self-giving spirit that many of us are afraid to try. You may call it magnanimity or generosity or bigness or graciousness or selflessness or unconditional love. Whatever label you put on it, Jesus is saying, "Live in this spirit ...."; and that's where the real difficulty begins. He is saying, "Respond to harshness with kindness," "Respond to cruelty with tenderness," "Respond to hurt with forgiveness," "Respond to adversity with perseverance," "Respond to hate with love."

Can Jesus really mean this? The world scoffs at this and says with the disciples in John's Gospel, "Wait a minute, now. This is more than we can stomach. How can we listen to this? There must be some mistake here. Life doesn't work that way." But don't you see? Jesus is saying that this is precisely the way life will work, if only we would be bold enough to believe it and try it. A soft answer does indeed turn away wrath. (If you don't believe it, go try it!) Forgiveness is indeed better than vengeance, every time. Love is indeed the most powerful thing in all the world. The only way you and I can be real, authentic disciples of Christ is to believe that and to stake our lives on it and to give our lives to it. To live in this gracious spirit is the calling of every Christian. It is the main message of the Sermon on the Mount. Read Matthew chapters 5, 6, and 7. You will see it there. Over and over Jesus hammers that message home to us: "Live in this spirit; live in this unselfish, gracious, forgiving spirit."

The real difficulty here is not so much in understanding what Jesus said—"Love your enemies. Pray for those who persecute you"—we know what that means. The difficulty is that we are not so sure we want to *do* it. The real difficulty comes when we understand that Jesus meant what he said. He meant it so much that he gave his life for it. He meant it so much that he saw these sacrificial qualities as the most authentic marks of Christian discipleship. The real difficulty here is in believing what Jesus said enough to try it.

Well, what do you think? Do you believe what Jesus taught enough to try it? Do his teachings still work? Do they fit in today's world? Jesus' teachings are beautiful, even provocative, but are they practical in a world like ours, a world that is hard-nosed and cynical, callous, power-hungry, and sometimes even violent? Going the second mile ... laying down the sword ... being meek ... loving one's enemies; what possible relevance do such soft-sounding attitudes have for this hard, tough world in which we live?

There has been a lot of discussion about this over the years. Brilliant scholars have debated it. Some scholars say, "These principles may work in personal life, but not in international affairs." Others say it's an "interim ethic," that Jesus felt the end of the world was coming soon, and he was giving us a way to live in those "final days" before the end of time. Still others say that Jesus meant what he said, just like he said it, and the problem is that we don't have the courage to try it.

Well, what do *you* think? Do you believe Jesus meant it? Are you willing to try it? Now, to get at this, let's be more specific. Let's look at one of the hardest-to-swallow things Jesus said: "Turn the other cheek." Remember how Jesus put it in Matthew 5: "You have heard that it was said, 'An eye for an eye and a tooth for a tooth.' But I say to you, Do not resist an evildoer. But if anyone strikes you on the right cheek, turn the other also" (Matt. 5:38-39). "Turn the other cheek"; what in the world is Jesus talking about here? What can this mean?

Let me suggest a few ideas for us to try on for size. Here's number one:

When Jesus Says, "Turn the Other Cheek," He Means "Don't Retaliate"

In other words, don't return hurt for hurt. Two wrongs don't make a right. Don't feel that when someone hurts you that you have got to get even. Jesus himself lived out this philosophy of "bigness of spirit." These are not just idle, idealistic words, but rather they represent the lifestyle of the Christian, the spirit of magnanimity and grace. Jesus suffered lots of hurts, lots of blows and insults of all kinds, but he never retaliated. He was too big for that.

Remember that famous old story about the two farmers who lived side by side. One day, the fence between the two farms was pushed down, and the livestock of one farmer got into the garden of the other farmer. The farmer whose garden was damaged was irate. He was so upset that he rounded up the other man's animals and refused to return them until the owner had paid in full for the damages. The farmer whose livestock had caused the problem apologized, gladly paid for the damages, took his cows home, and repaired the fence.

A few days later, ironically, the opposite thing happened. The other farmer's livestock pushed the fence down and got over into the garden of the farmer who had earlier had to pay damages. But this farmer, who now had this golden opportunity to retaliate, chose to come at the problem a different way. He rounded up the other man's cows and returned them to their owner. The owner, red-faced and embarrassed, reached for his checkbook and said, "I suppose you have the damages figured, so let me pay you and get it over with. How much do I owe you?"

"Nothing, nothing at all. Not a penny," said the kind farmer. "We are neighbors, and I'd much rather lose my garden than your friendship."

Later that night, there was a knock at the door of this kind farmer. When he opened the door, there stood his neighbor with the money he had received for damages a few days before. Handing over the money, the neighbor said, "Take it back. Please, take the money back. You've got something I don't have, and I want it: I want to find that kind of unselfish spirit. Maybe this will get me started."

Now, *that's* what it means to "turn the other cheek," to not retaliate. This does *not* mean to be negative or passive or namby-pamby. It doesn't mean to be weak. On the contrary, to turn the other cheek means *strength*. Anybody can lose their temper. Anybody can be selfish. Anybody can demand their "pound of flesh." But it takes a special person, a special spirit, a special strength to respond positively and lovingly, out of bigness.

The Christian disciple never retaliates.

When Jesus Says, "Turn the Other Cheek," He Also Means "Don't Resent"

There is nothing more paralyzing or devastating to our spiritual lives than resentment. There is nothing that can make you sadder *quicker* than resentment. There is nothing that can make you more miserable than resentment. The dangerous thing about resentment is that it can creep into the lives of good people. People who would never rob a bank or murder a person can become the victim of resentment.

In his commentary on Matthew, William Barclay puts the emphasis here. Barclay says that when Jesus says, "Turn the other cheek," there is far more here than meets the eye, far more than a mere matter of blows to the face. Barclay says, "Suppose a right-handed man is standing in front of another man, and suppose he wants to slap the other man on the right cheek, how must he do it? ... *with the back of his hand.* Now according to Jewish Rabbinic Law, to hit a man with the *back* of the hand was twice as insulting as to hit him with the *flat* of the hand.... So, then, what Jesus is saying is this: 'Even if a man should direct at you the most deadly and calculated insult, you must on no account ... resent it' " (William Barclay, *The Daily Study Bible: The Gospel of Matthew, vol. 1* [Philadelphia: Westminster Press, 1958], p. 166).

Now, not too many of us get slapped around physically, but time and again, life does bring us insults.

The true Christian has forgotten what it is to be insulted. Let me tell you something. When we start thinking, *Should I be personally offended by what someone has said or done?* When we begin to think of that, *should I be personally offended,* at that moment, we have departed from the Spirit of Christ. As Christians, we learn from our Master how to accept any insult and never resent it, to turn the other cheek and go on with life.

When Jesus says, "Turn the other cheek," he means don't retaliate and don't resent.

When Jesus Says, "Turn the Other Cheek," He Also Means "Don't Quit"

When someone, or life itself, hurts us or knocks us down, we can respond in several different ways. We can try to get even, demanding our "pound of flesh"; we can build a thick protective shell and try to hide behind it; we can quit on life and try to run away; or we can "turn the other cheek"—that is, we can get back up and dust ourselves off, stick out our chin again, and go on living creatively and confidently.

I saw a cartoon recently that made me chuckle. It was a picture of a little boy, six or seven years old, sitting in a corner, obviously being disciplined by his parents. He turns his head just slightly and mutters out of the side of his mouth these words: "*Outside* I may be sitting down, but *inside* I'm standing up!" Maybe that's what it means to "turn the other cheek"—to have that kind of spirit that will not quit.

Some years ago, a young Christian woman was arrested and put in jail because she dared to stand up for her faith in Christ. More than that, she was put in solitary confinement and placed in an antiquated, despicable cell with no windows and nothing more than a single lightbulb hanging on a cord in the middle of the room. She was harassed and vilified by her captors day and night.

And then one night, the jailer came with a pistol in his hand, shot out the lone lightbulb in her cell, and left the woman in total darkness. "Now we have taken away your light!" he cackled through the darkness. "*Now* what will you do?" With courage and firmness, she answered: "You cannot take away my light. God is my light, and because he is with me, I will never be in the darkness."

Can *you* say that? Can you say, "I will never be in the darkness, I will never give up, because God is with me. He is my light and my strength." That's also what it means to "turn the other cheek"—to stick out your chin, to trust God and to refuse to quit.

Don't Forget That When Jesus Says, "Turn the Other Cheek," He Means That "Love Is the Most Powerful Thing in the World"

Love is more powerful than physical force. When you stop and think about it, this "turn the other cheek" verse is a summary of Jesus' life. From the outset, Jesus was the victim of all kinds of hurts—insults, lies, gossip, prejudices, slander—slapped out at him, He was cursed and maligned, beaten and stripped and spat upon. He was nailed to a cross, and yet when they arrested him, Jesus never retaliated. When Peter drew his sword to defend Jesus, Jesus told Peter to lay down his sword.

Jesus never resented. He said from the cross, "Father forgive them." He never quit. He said, rather, "Not my will but thine be done," and, "Into thy hands I commit my spirit" (Luke 22:42; 23:46 NEB). Jesus just turned the other cheek and kept on loving. And then, when he died, the Roman centurion who had watched him through it all felt Jesus' love and summed it up when he said, "Truly this man was a son of God" (Matt. 27:54 NEB). Many years later, another soldier saw the same thing in Jesus. Napoleon, of all people, put it like this:

"Alexander, Caesar, Charlemagne, and myself founded empires; but on what foundation did we rest the creations of our genius? Upon force. Jesus Christ founded an empire upon love; and at this hour millions of men would die for him."

"Turn the other cheek," Jesus said. What does that mean? It means that when hurt comes, when life strikes you a hard blow, don't retaliate, don't resent, don't quit, and don't forget that love is the most powerful, the most godlike thing in all the world. "Turn the other cheek"; what does it mean? It means quite simply to live in the spirit of Christ.

Let me ask you something: Won't *you* try that? Won't you try that diligently for one day? If you will try it, to live in that spirit for one day, it will change your life forever.

12

The Promise of the Bible

Superstars, Smug Spectators, and Sacrificial Servants

2 TIMOTHY 3:10-17

Now you have observed my teaching, my conduct, my aim in life, my faith, my patience, my love, my steadfastness, my persecutions and suffering the things that happened to me in Antioch, Iconium, and Lystra. What persecutions I endured! Yet the Lord rescued me from all of them. Indeed, all who want to live a godly life in Christ Jesus will be persecuted. But wicked people and imposters will go from bad to worse, deceiving others and being deceived.

But as for you, continue in what you have learned and firmly believed, knowing from whom you learned it, and how from childhood you have known the sacred writings that are able to instruct you for salvation through faith in Christ Jesus. All scripture is inspired by God and is useful for teaching, for reproof, for correction, and for training in righteousness, so that everyone who belongs to God may be proficient, equipped for every good work.

In September of 1991, death claimed one of the most beloved writers of our time. His real name was Theodor

Geisel, but he was affectionately known to the world by his pen name, Dr. Seuss. He was, of course, the celebrated author of numerous wonderful children's books: *The Cat in the Hat, Horton Hears a Who!, Green Eggs & Ham,* and *The Grinch Who Stole Christmas,* among others.

A few years ago, Dr. Seuss was invited to give the Commencement address at a college in Illinois. As he stood to face those excited graduates, he said, "It seems behooven upon me to bring forth great words of wisdom ... to this graduating class as it leaves these cloistered halls to enter the outside world.... However, my wisdom is in rather short supply ... so I have managed to condense everything I know into this epic poem consisting of fourteen lines."

Dr. Seuss then recited his "epic poem," "On Eating Popovers":

> My uncle Terwilliger ordered popovers
> from the restaurant's bill of fare.
> And, when they were served, he regarded them
> with a penetrating stare.
> Then he spoke great words of Wisdom
> as he sat there on that chair:
> "To eat these things," said my uncle,
> "You must exercise great care.
> You may swallow down what's solid ...
> But you must spit out the air!"
> And ... as you partake of the world's bill of fare,
> that's darned good advice to follow.
> Do a lot of spitting out the hot air.
> And be careful what you swallow.

Now, that's certainly good advice, isn't it—not only for a group of graduating seniors, but indeed, for all of us.

There's a lot of hot air blowing around out there in the world these days. Strange notions, weird ideas, even dangerous religions are out there, vying for our attention and pleading for our allegiance. Dr. Seuss is right! We do need to be very careful what we swallow.

And he is not the first to tell us this. Way back in New Testament times, we find a warning from the writer of Second Timothy. He tells us it's a tough world out there, and we are going to be persecuted and taunted and tempted. But don't give up! And don't be taken in! And be very careful what you swallow! He gives us that warning, and then he gives us this advice:

> But as for you, continue in what you have learned and firmly believed, knowing from whom you learned it, and how from childhood you have known the sacred writings that are able to instruct you for salvation through faith in Christ Jesus. All scripture is inspired by God and is useful for teaching, for reproof, for correction, and for training in righteousness, so that everyone who belongs to God may be proficient, equipped for every good work. (2 Tim. 3:14-17)

In other words, let the Bible be your strength, your guide, your measuring stick for truth. When all those opposing ideas and causes and programs and beliefs come exploding in upon you, pulling you in every direction, competing for your attention, your dollars, and your loyalty, let the Bible be your measuring stick, your compass, and your barometer. Let the great themes of the Scriptures be the means by which you assess what is true and right and valuable and good. Let me illustrate this.

Some years ago, there was a great professor at Centenary College, Dean R. E. Smith, a very distinctive looking man who wore a black patch over one eye. Dean Smith was a saintly man, a brilliant scholar, an outstanding communicator, a real friend to the students, really a legend in his own time.

Standing on the Promises or Sitting on the Premises?

In one of his most famous lectures, Dean Smith would talk to his students about how we can discover truth, how we determine what is genuine and authentic. After some discussion, Dean Smith would suddenly ask the students, "How wide is my desk?" The students would look at the desk and then make their best guesses. A variety of answers would ring out.

"I think it's about 72 inches wide."

"No, I believe it's more like 68 inches wide."

"Looks like 75 to me."

"I'm going to guess 74 inches."

Then some wise guy from the back of the room would say, "71 and 5/16?" and everyone would laugh.

Then Dean Smith would say, "These are all pretty good guesses, but one of them is more nearly true than the others. Now, how do we determine which one is most accurate? How do we decide which answer is most nearly right?"

There would be complete silence for a moment in the classroom, and then someone would say tentatively, "Get a measuring stick?"

"That's right," Dean Smith would say. "To determine which one is closest to the truth, we have to get a measuring stick and measure it!"

Then he would go to the blackboard. He would take a piece of chalk, and, in silence, draw the outline of a cross. With the chalk, he would trace over and over the outline of the cross, letting it dramatically sink into the hearts and minds of those students.

Then he would stand back, point to that cross, and say, "There's your measuring stick! There's your measuring stick for truth!"

With the Bible comes God's encouraging promise: "Here's your compass. Here's your guiding light. Here's your measuring stick for truth. Study the Bible. Memorize its key verses. Get the Scriptures inside you. Write them on your heart. Immerse yourselves in the

Bible. Learn the key themes of the Bible. And the Bible will be your measuring stick, to show you what is true and right and good."

If the world today says it's OK to steal, remember what the Bible says about that. If the world today says it's not so bad to lie, remember what the Bible says about that. If the world today says it's not so important to be faithful anymore, remember what the Bible says about that. If the world today tells you it's OK to cheat or hurt or gossip or hate or hold a grudge, remember what the Bible says. Remember the cross!

The measuring stick of the Bible tells us to be committed to Christ and compassionate toward others, to be loving and caring and kind, to be just and honest and truthful, to be loyal and merciful and gracious. Anything that doesn't measure up to those instructions is wrong and sinful! There are so many great truths in the Bible, but let me underscore one case and show you how it plays out in our modern world.

The Bible Clearly Teaches Us That We Are Called to Be Servants

Servants—not privileged people, not pampered people, not passive people, not holier-than-thou people, but servant people! On page after page after page of the Bible, we hear these commands: Serve! Love! Give yourself! Reach out to others with help and healing! Be God's servants! Sacrifice yourself! We hear that theme all through the Scriptures. And yet deep down inside, we wonder, Does God really mean that? Does God really mean *me*? Does God want me to be a servant? Does God want me to sacrifice? Does God really mean that?

Well, Jesus showed us that he meant it—on a cross! But still, the plain fact is that much of the world turns a deaf ear to that biblical call. We see that vividly by the ways people view and perceive themselves today.

115

Some years ago, Philip Yancey wrote a fascinating article about servant leaders, "Low Pay, Long Hours, No Applause," which appeared in *Christianity Today*. In that article, he made a perceptive observation about the source of personal fulfillment. He said that in his career as a writer and journalist, he had interviewed all kinds of people. He divides them roughly into two groups—the stars and the servants.

Interestingly, and ironically, Philip Yancey expresses sympathy for the stars, those famous people who are in the limelight and receive a lot of recognition and applause. He feels sorry for them. So many of them, he says, are unhappy: "These idols are as miserable a group of people as I have ever met." They seem to have more personal problems, more troubled psyches, more incurable self-doubts than most other people. His point is clear. Their self-indulgent, self-centered, pampered lifestyle will not work; it is not fulfilling.

On the other hand, Yancey discovered that people who see themselves not as stars, but as servants, are radiantly happy. Relief workers in Bangladesh; mission workers in Costa Rica; community volunteers; Ph.D.s scattered through the jungles of South America, translating the Bible into obscure languages—in these people, he sees an indescribable joy, strength, and serenity.

Then Philip Yancey says a fascinating thing: "I was prepared to honor and admire these servants, to uphold them as inspiring examples, but what surprised me was that I found myself envying them!" He concluded with this:

> As I now reflect on these two groups, the stars and the servants, the servants clearly emerge as the favored ones, the graced ones. They work for low pay, long hours, and no applause, [giving away] their talents among the poor and uneducated. But somehow, in the process of losing their lives, they have found them.

Does that sound at all familiar? It should! This is precisely what Jesus said, 2,000 years ago: "For those who want to save their life will lose it, and those who lose their life for my sake, and for the sake of the gospel, will save it."

Now, let me ask you—How do you see yourself right now? How do you perceive yourself?

- Do you see yourself as a Superstar, one who expects to be catered to and pampered, one who wants lots of perks and applause, one whose major interest in life is indulgence?
- Or do you see yourself as a Smug Spectator, one who never really gets on the playing field, but is content to sit complacently on the sidelines and critique and criticize what others are trying to do?
- Or do you see yourself as a Sacrificial Servant, one who hears God's call to service and says, "Here am I, Lord, send me," one who is willing to roll up your sleeves, take up the cross, and do God's work in this world?

You know what the Bible says about this, don't you? The Bible clearly calls us to be servants—sacrificial servants, self-giving servants. We must never forget that.

A few years ago, my friend Clarence Forsberg attended a meeting of the American Booksellers Association, where he met a number of well-known writers and celebrities. One of them was Muhammad Ali, who was there to autograph his new autobiography, *The Greatest: My Own Story.* Ali was signing all his books with the inscription, "I am the greatest!"

At a press conference later, a sports writer asked him, "Ali, when you say you are the greatest, do you mean the greatest fighter, or the greatest human being?"

Ali quickly replied, "I mean the greatest boxer. I will go down in history as the greatest boxer of all time."

But the sports writer persisted: "But do you think that fifty years from now, people will say that you were the greatest?"

Ali replied, "Fifty years from now, everybody in this room will be dead. Nobody will remember what a great boxer I was. The truth is that the only way I will not be forgotten is if I can do something to help people."

This is something of a Christian parable for us, because when all is said and done, the only things that really matter are those things we do for God and for God's children. That is why the Bible does not call us to be stars or spectators, but repeatedly calls us to be sacrificial servants. And with that call to sacrifice comes a great promise. If we will take up the cross of Christ and live in his spirit, if we will live in the spirit of sacrificial service, our lives will be full and joyous and meaningful! That's a promise.

13

The Promise of New Life

Launch Out into the Deep

LUKE 5:1-11

Once while Jesus was standing beside the lake of Gennesaret, and the crowd was pressing in on him to hear the word of God, he saw two boats there at the shore of the lake; the fishermen had gone out of them and were washing their nets. He got into one of the boats, the one belonging to Simon, and asked him to put out a little way from the shore. Then he sat down and taught the crowds from the boat.

When he had finished speaking, he said to Simon, "Put out into the deep water and let down your nets for a catch." Simon answered, "Master, we have worked all night long but have caught nothing. Yet if you say so, I will let down the nets." When they had done this, they caught so many fish that their nets were beginning to break. So they signaled their partners in the other boat to come and help them. And they came and filled both boats, so that they began to sink.

But when Simon Peter saw it, he fell down at Jesus' knees, saying, "Go away from me, Lord, for I am a sinful man!" For he and all who were with him were amazed at the catch of fish that they had

119

*taken; and so also were James and John, sons of
Zebedee, who were partners with Simon. Then
Jesus said to Simon, "Do not be afraid; from now on
you will be catching people." When they had
brought their boats to shore, they left everything
and followed him.*

Let me share with you a poignant story from Arthur
Gordon's *A Touch of Wonder.* He tells about a bleak period in his life when everything seemed stale and flat. His
enthusiasm was gone. His energy was waning. He felt
tired and listless and bored most of the time. There was
no zest or joy in his life.

He was smart enough to realize that he was in trouble,
that his spirit was dying, so he went to a doctor for help.

"Doctor," he said, "I don't know what's wrong with
me. I just seem to have come to a dead end. I'm not
happy. I'm just going through the motions. I'm not creative and productive, like I used to be. The radiance and
excitement are gone. Can you help me?"

The doctor gazed at him for a moment and said, "I
don't know, but let me ask, Where were you happiest as
a child?"

Without hesitation, Arthur Gordon replied, "At the
beach. We had a cottage there. We loved the water, the
ocean."

Then the doctor said, "Are you capable of following
instructions?"

Arthur Gordon answered, "I think so."

"All right. Here's what I want you to do. I want you to
drive to the beach alone tomorrow morning, not later
than nine in the morning. You may take a lunch with
you, but I don't want you to read or write or listen to the
radio or talk to anyone. And here are four prescriptions.
I want you to take one every three hours, at 9 in the
morning, 12 noon, 3 P.M. and 6 P.M."

Arthur Gordon said to the doctor, "Are you serious?"

The doctor laughed and replied, "Wait till you get my bill, and you'll see how serious I am!"

The next morning, Arthur Gordon drove to the beach and, at 9 o'clock, opened the first prescription. It said: "Listen carefully." At first, he wasn't sure what that meant. What was there to listen to? There was no one to talk to, no radio on. But then he began to hear the sound of the wind in the grass, the ocean surf breaking on the beach, the call of the seagulls—the sounds of creation.

He thought to himself, "Yes! Yes! I'm part of this," and as he listened and reflected on what he heard, the three hours passed quickly.

It was noon. Time to open up the second prescription. This one had three words written on it: "Try Reaching Back."

"Now, what does that mean?" he said to himself with some agitation. "Try reaching back." Arthur Gordon's mind went back in time. He thought about his past, his childhood, the happy times, the good times. He had so much to be thankful for, so much in his life that was rich and valuable. And again, the three hours flew by quickly and easily as he enjoyed his reflections on the past.

Then it was 3 o'clock in the afternoon, and time for the third prescription. He opened it, and again found three words: "Reexamine Your Motives."

Now, this made him angry and he said to himself, "Wait just a minute. Who does that doctor think he is, telling me, of all people, to reexamine my motives? I'm a good man. I've done some worthwhile things with my life. I'm not hurting anyone or destroying anything. Why should I reexamine my motives?"

It took a while to work through the anger, but then suddenly he realized that maybe his motives weren't as clear as he thought they were. Possibly they had slipped a bit from where they had been when he had a purpose for writing. Maybe now he was just writing for money, to get the job done, without any real purpose or enthusiasm.

And then he thought, "Yes, I do need to reexamine my motives."

The sun was starting to set and the day was coming to an end, and now it was 6 o'clock—time to take the fourth and final prescription. He opened it and found these words: "Write Your Worries in the Sand!" As the tide was coming in, Arthur Gordon knelt down and wrote his worries in the sand. And then he watched as the tide came in and washed them away.

That day was a day of healing for Arthur Gordon. As he listened carefully to the sounds of creation, reached back to his roots, reexamined his motives, and then wrote his worries in the sand, he had come to realize his problem. His life had lost its joy and zest because he had been wading in the shallows and missing the depths; he had been muddling with mundane things and missing the magnificence of life.

Arthur Gordon went home that day a new man, with a joy unspeakable, a renewed sense of purpose, a restored sense of direction, and an exciting sense of mission—ready to start his life over again. On the beach that day, God had walked into his life in a fresh new way, and Arthur Gordon had been reborn!

(Adapted from *A Touch of Wonder* [Grand Rapids: Fleming H. Revell Co., Baker Book House, 1984].)

His experience reminds me of another beach scene when rebirth took place. It's recorded in Luke 5. Here we see Simon, James, and John fishing along the shore of Lake Gennesaret. They are professional fishermen, and they are tired and worn, discouraged and disappointed because they have fished all night and have caught nothing at all.

Jesus is so perceptive, he sizes up the situation quickly, sees their problem, empathizes with him, and points to a solution. He says, "You're too shallow! Launch out into the deep and let down your nets."

"But Master," Simon answers, "we have worked all night and have caught nothing. The fish aren't biting. We're ready to quit, but if you say so, we'll give it another try."

They followed Jesus' lead, did precisely what he told them to do. They launched out into deeper water, let down their nets, and—can you believe it? They caught so many fish their nets began to break, so many they had to call other boats to help bring in all the fish! Simon was so astonished by the power of the Master, he felt unworthy to be in the presence of such greatness.

So he rushed to shore, fell at the feet of Jesus, and cried out, "Go away from me, Lord, for I am a sinful man." But Jesus lifted Simon up and called him to discipleship: "Come, Simon, and follow me. Do not be afraid; from now on you will be catching people." And Simon and James and John left everything and followed him.

Isn't that a wonderful story? There are so many things here we could talk about—the miracle catch, the call to discipleship, the significance of the seashore, the absence of Simon's brother, Andrew. (Where is he? Why is he not in the story?) There is the importance of obedience, of doing precisely what the Master tells us to do. There are the unique elements of this story as it's recorded here in Luke 5, elements not found in Matthew, Mark, or John. There is the sense of unworthiness that Simon felt in the powerful presence of Jesus.

All these things are important, and they deserve our thought, but just now, I want us to realize that we need to launch out into the deep and discover the new birth that comes as Christ takes us out of the shallows and into the depths of life and faith. His word to us in this passage rings loud and clear. Can you hear him? Can you hear him calling your name, saying, "Launch out into the deep! You've been in the shallows long enough. Push out into the deep, and find new life!"

Let me be more specific with the following thoughts.

We Can Launch Out into the Depths of Gratitude

When Simon saw that incredible catch of fish that Christ had blessed them with, he was filled with gratitude. I can just hear him saying with the psalmist, "Bless the LORD, O my Soul, and all that is within me, bless his holy name! Bless the LORD, O my soul, and do not forget all his benefits" (Ps. 103:1-2). That is the song of genuine thanksgiving, and yet so often, the song goes unsung, doesn't it? We have so much to be thankful for, and yet the truth is that we do forget God's goodness. We do take for granted God's blessings. We do become unmindful of God's generosity.

The noted journalist John Gile writes about this in *Keeping First Things First*:

My four-year-old daughter has a magic body. I told her so. And it's true.

A few days ago she fell off a swing in a friend's yard and cut her hand. It didn't require major medical attention, just a quick washing, a small bandage, routine tear drying, and a few reassuring hugs.

But today we noticed something remarkable: the cut was gone, vanished without a trace. Somehow—like magic—her body had repaired the injured hand, making it like new again.

I know some cynics will come along and tell us it's not magic. They'll tell us that there's a Latin term for it and proceed to give us a boring description of the process.

But that doesn't take away the magic. It just explains how God makes "magic" things happen.

Our trouble is that sometimes we're too dull to recognize God's magic. Imagine if someone made a car that repaired its own dented fenders and scratched paint. The whole world would be excited about it. It would be featured on the news and make headlines around the world.

But God gives us a magic body and we just take it for granted—as we do with so many of [God's] gifts. Lord, please forgive us for being so dull....

The only surprising thing is that we are so slow to recognize and trust the One behind it all.
(Rockford, Ill.: John Gile Communications, 1990, pp. 10, 64.)

If we want a new lease on life, a new start, a new
beginning, a new birth, a new zestfulness, we can find all
that out there in the depths of gratitude. If we will reach
out and take Christ's hand, he will lead us into the deeper waters of thankfulness.

We Can Launch Out into the Depths of Penitence

First Simon felt gratitude, then penitence. He was so
awed and astonished by the amazing power of Jesus that
he felt unworthy to be in his presence. Like Moses at the
burning bush, he wanted to take off his shoes, for he
knew he stood on holy ground. Like Isaiah in the
Temple, he felt he was an unclean man with unclean
lips, dwelling in the midst of unclean people. In anguish,
Simon cried out, "Go away from me, Lord, for I am a sinful man."

Simon was rocked to the depths of his soul. In the
powerful presence of Christ, he felt sorrow for his sinful-
ness. He felt unclean and unworthy. It was a cry of
penitence.

In the Scriptures, penitence is a painful process, a
deeply moving experience. People cry, tear their clothes,
fall on their knees, and change their ways. But today, the
truth is that, more often than not, we treat sin so light-
ly; we just play around in the shallows of penitence.

For example, a few years ago, a writer named A. J.
Langguth told about a brazen young woman who felt that
she was demon-possessed. She believed that she had
seven demons within her. In the story, she is brought
before Jesus for healing. Jesus looks at her for a moment
and then says, "I can help you. I can cast out those seven
demons. Would you like that?"

To which the young woman replies, "Would you mind just casting out six?"

We understand that woman, don't we? There's something about us that wants to hold something back, doesn't want to release ourselves completely, that wants to repent and be a Christian only up to a point. So much of our penitence is halfhearted and shallow.

We are much like the man who became irate when the neighborhood children walked in his freshly poured concrete drive.

Finally, his wife said to him, "Why are you so angry? I thought you loved children."

"I do love children," he said, "but I love them in the abstract, not in the concrete!" Too often, we repent in the abstract; we don't become concrete enough. Penitence means being so sorry for our sins that we change completely.

In the Old Testament, the Hebrew word for "repent" is *hashivenu*, and it means "about face," "turn around," "change direction." If we want a new life, a new start, one place to find that new beginning is out there in the depths of penitence. Christ helps us to launch out into the depths of gratitude and into the depths of penitence.

We Can Launch Out into the Depths of Commitment

Simon, James, and John left everything and followed Jesus, and their commitment was so deep that they turned the world upside down—or maybe better, "right side up." When you stop and think about it, shallow commitment is not worth much at all, but deep commitment is one of the most powerful things in the world.

This is powerfully portrayed by a young soldier who was brought into a field hospital with a badly shattered arm. The surgeon had to amputate at the elbow.

When the young soldier came out of the anesthetic, the surgeon told him as gently as he could, "Son, I'm sorry, but we had to take your arm."

126

The soldier, although groggy and weak, still was able to say, "Sir, you did not take it. I gave it!" That's commitment, isn't it?

I can picture in my mind that scene from church tradition, when the Romans are taking Simon Peter to be executed because of his allegiance to Christ.

"Crucify me upside down," Simon told them. "I'm not worthy to be sacrificed like my Lord."

The centurion tells him: "But Simon, if you will deny Christ right now, we won't have to take your life. You will be spared."

Simon answers, "You are not taking my life. I'm giving it!"

That's what commitment is—self-giving! It's the giving of ourselves in complete devotion to Christ. Are you committed like that? Is your commitment that deep? We all need to hear and respond, in faith and obedience, to our Lord's Word for us today—launch out into the deep! Get out of the shallows! Launch out into the depths of gratitude and penitence and commitment. If we will launch out into the deep, God will give us new life. That's a promise!

14

The Promise of Prayer

___

How Do We Pray and Why?

LUKE 11:1-4

He was praying in a certain place, and after he had finished, one of his disciples said to him, "Lord, teach us to pray, as John taught his disciples." He said to them, "When you pray, say:
> *Father, hallowed be your name.*
> *Your kingdom come.*
> *Give us each day our daily bread.*
> *And forgive us our sins,*
> *for we ourselves forgive everyone*
>   *indebted to us.*
> *And do not bring us to the time of trial."*

Let me share with you one of my favorite stories. It's called the legend of the touchstone. It is not a true story, but it is a great "truth story," one that serves as a haunting parable for you and me.

According to the legend, if you could find the touchstone on the coast of the Black Sea and hold it in your hand, everything you touched while holding it would turn to gold. You could recognize the touchstone by its warmth. All the other stones would feel cold, but the touchstone, as you picked it up, would turn warm in your hand.

Once, a man sold everything he had and went to the Black Sea in search of the touchstone. He began picking up every stone he could find on the coastline, wanting desperately to find the touchstone. After some days passed, he realized he was picking up the same stones again and again. So, he devised a plan: Pick up a stone; if it's cold, throw it into the sea. This he did for weeks and weeks. But then one morning, he came out early to continue his search for the touchstone. He picked up a stone. It was cold, and he threw it into the sea. He picked up another, and it was cold. He threw it into the sea. He picked up another and another and another. They were all cold, and he threw each into the sea.

He then picked up yet another stone. It turned warm in his hand, but before he realized what he was doing, he threw it into the sea! He had it in his hand, and he threw it away. So dulled by the routine, he did not recognize that stone's specialness, and, absent-mindedly, he tossed it aside.

This can happen to us with the Lord's Prayer. We pick it up so often; we hear it so often. We repeat the words so often that if we are not careful, we miss the specialness, the power, the sacredness of the prayer. And before we even realize what we are doing, we throw it away, toss it aside, fling it into the sea; and that is so sad.

What a treasure the Lord's Prayer is! And we have it in our hands. Jesus gave it to us. Please don't treat it casually or carelessly. Please don't routinely toss it aside. It is a sacred gift from our Lord. Remember how it's recorded in the Bible. The disciples of Jesus came to him one day and said, "Lord, teach us to pray."

Notice something here. When did the disciples ask for this? When did they make this request? Was it after Jesus gave a lecture on prayer? No. Was it after Jesus led a seminar on prayer? No. Was it after Jesus preached a powerful sermon on prayer? No. None of these. Remember how Luke 11 describes it. Jesus "was praying in a certain place, and after he had finished, one of his disciples said to him, 'Lord, teach us to pray'" (Luke 11:1). The point is clear: They saw what prayer meant to him and what it did for him. They saw the amazing spiritual power released in him by prayer, and they wanted that too. So in response to their request, Jesus taught them the Lord's Prayer. What a treasure we have in our hands! Please, let's take care not to treat it casually or carelessly. Let's take care not to routinely mouth the words. It is a sacred gift.

Let me ask this question: As Jesus gives his disciples the Lord's Prayer, what does he teach them, and us, about prayer? Many things, of course, but for now let me lift up three lessons that have been supremely helpful to me in my prayer life. Are you ready? Here is number one.

Jesus Teaches Us to Pray in the Spirit of Gratitude

Jesus prayed, "Our Father which art in heaven, Hallowed be thy name ..."; "praise be to thy name ..."; "thanks be to thy name." If you spend time with Jesus, you will quickly and dramatically sense his incredible spirit of appreciation. If you draw close to him, you cannot miss his amazing spirit of thanksgiving and gratitude.

If someone called today and told us that we had just won a Mercedes-Benz automobile or a trip to Hawaii or twenty million dollars, we would probably be excited and grateful. But please notice that it is Jesus' enthusiasm for the little things—the seemingly ordinary and commonplace things—that really reveals his appreciative spirit.

Remember his frequent references to simple things like brooms, candles, leaven, old cloth, flowers, birds, mustard seeds, rocks, sunsets, the wind, the sky, the grass of the field, the faces of little children, and in the Lord's Prayer, our daily bread. These are the kinds of commonplace things that we too often take for granted. But all of these simple things spoke to Jesus and touched his heart and reminded him of the love and care of the Creator. He saw them as good and sacred gifts from the generous hand of our Father.

When you really stop to think about it, you realize that there is no such thing as an "ungrateful Christian." A Christian by definition is one who accepts Christ as his or her personal Savior and then lives daily in the Spirit of Christ. And that means to live daily in the spirit of gratitude.

Back in the early days of the church, a rather strong-smelling incense was burned in the worship services, and the aroma of that incense was so powerful that it would saturate the clothing of all who were present. When the people left the church, they literally smelled of incense. Now, think of that; wherever they went, other people could tell by their fragrance that they had been to church; people could tell by their aroma that they had been in the presence of God. Isn't that a beautiful thought? Well, today the fragrance of Christians is "gratitude"—unconditional gratitude, gratitude in all circumstances, because come what may, God loves us and God is with us and God will see us through.

Let me ask you something: Can people sense the fragrance of gratitude in you? That's what happens to us when we really come into the presence of Christ. It changes us because we have been exposed to a higher standard. Our sloppy ways of selfishly grumbling and griping and complaining just don't feel right anymore because we have been exposed to his great spirit, to his high standard of appreciation and thanksgiving and gratitude.

Now, listen closely. I want to give you the greatest definition of prayer I have ever heard. It is so simple and yet so profound. Here it is: *Prayer is friendship with God.* If you will remember that, it will change your life, and it will change the way you pray. If prayer is, simply put, friendship with God, then that means we can talk to God the same way we talk to our best friend. We can lay out our fears, our concerns, our worries, our successes, our disappointments, our problems, our joys, our sorrows, and our dreams and know that God will understand and will love us and help us and support us come what may, because he is our Best Friend. But I also believe that whatever we bring to God, we should bring it in the spirit of gratitude. In the Lord's Prayer, Jesus teaches us that we should pray in the spirit of gratitude.

Jesus Teaches Us to Pray in the Spirit of Forgiveness

Right in the middle of the Lord's Prayer we find these words: "Forgive us our trespasses, as we forgive those who trespass against us." Jesus is teaching us again the crucial lesson about forgiveness that he taught so often and that we need so desperately to hear and understand, namely, that we need to be forgiven and we need to be forgivers.

We accept God's forgiveness, and then we pass that forgiveness on to others. We receive forgiveness from our Lord, and then we become "echoes" of his forgiving spirit in the world. Or, put another way, we cannot come fully into the presence of God with hatred and hostility in our hearts.

Remember how Jesus put this so dramatically in the Sermon on the Mount. He said that if you come to the altar and remember that someone has something against you, go fix that, go reconcile that, and then come back to the altar. But you may say, "Now, wait a minute; it's not *my* fault!" Of course it's not your fault, but as a Christian it is your responsibility to fix it because the spiritual poisons of hatred, hostility, resentment, and bitterness will contaminate your spirit and devastate your soul.

Let me show you what I mean. One of Leonardo da Vinci's most famous creations is his painting of the Lord's Supper. It is said that while da Vinci was working on the painting, he got into an argument with a fellow painter. Da Vinci was so mad at this colleague that, in anger and out of spite, he used that man's face as the face of Judas in his painting.

But then, having completed Judas's face, da Vinci turned to paint the face of Christ, and he could not do it. It would not come; he could not visualize it. He could not paint the face of Christ. He put down his paintbrush, and he went to find his enemy and to forgive him. They reconciled with one another. They both apologized, and they both forgave. That very evening da Vinci had a dream, and in that dream he saw the face of Christ. He rose quickly from his bed and finished the painting, and it became one of his greatest masterpieces.

The point is this: Leonardo da Vinci could not portray the face of Christ with hostility in his heart. And neither can we! We come to God for our forgiveness. Then we are called to live in his generous, gracious, forgiving Spirit.

In the Lord's Prayer, Jesus teaches us to pray in the spirit of gratitude and in the spirit of forgiveness.

Jesus Teaches Us to Pray in the Spirit of Trust

Jesus put it like this: "Lead us not into temptation, but deliver us from evil: For thine is the kingdom, and the power, and the glory, for ever" (Matt. 6:13 KJV)—which meant, "O Lord, you are the King of Life forever, so we will trust you and follow your lead."

A few summers ago our family spent some of our vacation time at a cabin in Beaver Creek, Colorado. One afternoon, our grandson Paul and I went for a walk in the mountains. We had a great time. He was three-and-a-half years old at the time, and he has always been a delight to be with.

We saw squirrels and rabbits and birds and prairie dogs and fish and turtles. We saw beautiful Aspen trees and magnificent wildflowers. We skipped rocks across the surface of the amazing Eagle River. Together we just soaked up the sights and sounds and fragrances of those incredible mountains.

When it was time to head back, I asked Paul a series of questions: "Paul, do you know how to get back? Do you know where the cabin is? Do you know which way to go?"

"No sir," he answered.

Then, I said to him, "Are you lost?"

"No, Gran," he said, "I can't be lost, 'cause I'm with you!"

Now, *that* is the picture of trust, isn't it? "I can't be lost, 'cause I'm with you." Let me ask you something: Do *you* trust anybody like that? Do you trust anybody that much? Do you trust God like a little child? This is what Jesus had in mind when he said, "Unless you become like a little child, you cannot enter the kingdom of God" (Matt. 18:3).

If we could pray to God each day with that kind of childlike trust, it would make all the difference. If we could really know God as a loving, caring parent who knows what's best for us, then every prayer and every day would be entrusted to him and to the doing of his will. As one of my saintly older friends puts it in her prayers, "Now, Lord, here's what I would like ..." Then she would give her specific list—*I want this or that or the other*—But then she would conclude by saying, "Have it your way, Lord, 'cause you're a lot smarter than I am."

In the Lord's Prayer, Jesus teaches us to pray always in the spirit of gratitude, in the spirit of forgiveness, and in the spirit of trust.

15

The Promise of Compassion

Ways to Express Love

LUKE 19:1-10

He entered Jericho and was passing through it. A man was there named Zacchaeus; he was a chief tax collector and was rich. He was trying to see who Jesus was, but on account of the crowd he could not, because he was short in stature. So he ran ahead and climbed a sycamore tree to see him, because he was going to pass that way. When Jesus came to the place, he looked up and said to him, "Zacchaeus, hurry and come down; for I must stay at your house today."

So he hurried down and was happy to welcome him. All who saw it began to grumble and said, "He has gone to be the guest of one who is a sinner." Zacchaeus stood there and said to the Lord, "Look, half of my possessions, Lord, I will give to the poor, and if I have defrauded anyone of anything, I will pay back four times as much." Then Jesus said to him, "Today salvation has come to this house, because he too is a son of Abraham. For the Son of Man came to seek out and to save the lost."

Don Locker, pastor of First United Methodist Church in Glendale, California, tells a delightful story about a vivacious older woman in his congregation. When she reached her mid-eighties, she decided to enter a retirement home. She had a number of close friends who already lived there, and they decided to give her a welcome party. They planned a beautiful banquet and seated her at the place of honor at the head table.

Immediately, she noticed that seated next to her was an older gentleman, quite dignified, well-dressed, and strikingly handsome, also in his eighties. He had lived in the retirement home for some time. When she sat down beside him, she stared and stared at him until it became a little obvious and embarrassing.

Finally, she said, "Please forgive me for staring at you like this, but I can't help it. You see, you look exactly like my third husband!"

"Oh," he responded. "How many times have you been married?"

With a warm smile and a twinkle in her eye, she patted his hand and answered, "Twice!"

Now, there's a lady who knows how to express love. Sadly, however, she is in the minority. The unfortunate fact is that so many people never learn, in a whole lifetime, how to express their love. Sociologists, psychologists, and anthropologists have been telling us for years that love is learned. It isn't something that just happens spontaneously. But the question is: Who teaches us to love?

Leo Buscaglia has been trying desperately to bring this to our attention in his books and lectures. He says we teach children facts. We teach them how to read and write and how to do math, but we assume that they know how to love, so we leave to chance the most important thing of all.

Recently I visited with a young minister from one of our western states about a new program he started in his church last year. He calls the program "Honesty at All Costs." Modeled somewhat after the "sensitivity movement" of the sixties, the purpose of the program is to bring together small groups of eight to ten people, to teach them how to relate to one another in total honesty.

On the surface that sounds okay, but as he described the experience, one thing that young minister said really bothered me. He reported that "the most significant accomplishment of the program is that people are learning how to express openly and candidly the hostilities they feel toward each other." And then he added, "And that, more than anything else, is what they need to learn."

Well, I don't know about you, but I don't agree with that. Now, I know about *The Angry Book* that came out a few years ago, and I know that we need to express our hostilities, rather than nurse them and let them fester within. But I don't believe for a minute that most people (more than anything else) need to learn how to express their hostilities. The world is already pretty expert at that. What we need most of all is to learn how to express our *love.*

There is so much love in this world, all bottled up in the hearts of people who don't know how to express it. The most unhappy people I know are much more adept at expressing their animosities. They are specialists at that. What they don't know is how to express love. The ability to express love is so important and so powerful. We see that vividly in Luke 19, as Jesus reaches out to Zacchaeus. Remember the story with me.

Jesus and his disciples were going to Jerusalem, and as they came to Jericho, a great crowd gathered to see him. Zacchaeus was in the crowd. The Scriptures tell us that Zacchaeus was a chief tax collector and rich, and he was disliked by the people of Jericho—for a number of reasons.

For one thing, Zacchaeus was responsible for gathering the hated Roman tax on the products of Jericho, such as balsam, and upon the costly imports from Damascus and Arabia. In the day of Jesus, tax collectors were known for their greed; they were considered outcasts and classed with thieves and cutthroats.

Also, Zacchaeus was regarded by the people of Jericho as a traitor. He was a fellow Jew, working with and for the enemy. They saw him as one who had betrayed his people, his nation, his faith, and his God. To them, he was a turncoat who had become rich at their expense. He had "cashed in" on their misfortune. So they shunned him, rejected him.

This was the setting when Jesus came to Jericho that day. There was a lot of hostility toward Zacchaeus in the air. The townspeople knew well how to express that. But then along came Jesus, to show them how to express love.

Jesus spotted Zacchaeus up in that sycamore tree. He quickly sized up the situation. How perceptive Jesus was! He felt the animosity aimed at Zacchaeus. He sensed his loneliness, and his heart went out to him.

Jesus went over, looked up, and said, "Zacchaeus, hurry and come down; for I must stay at your house today." That was a high compliment!

Zacchaeus, overwhelmed by the Master's acceptance of him and by this special honor, and touched powerfully by his love, jumped down quickly and welcomed Jesus warmly. And because of that tender moment of love and grace, Zacchaeus's whole life was changed. That one expression of love turned his life around.

Notice that Jesus gave him no material gifts. He gave him something much better—love, respect, and acceptance. Zacchaeus was so profoundly moved that his whole lifestyle was totally changed. Why, it even touched his pocketbook!

"Look, half of my possessions, Lord," he said, "I will give to the poor, and if I have defrauded anyone of anything, I will pay back four times as much."

That's what genuine love does. It changes our lives.

We receive God's love, and then we have to pass it on to others. Now, look at what happened. Jesus showed us specifically that day in Jericho some of the most effective and meaningful ways to express love.

Love Can Be Expressed with Words

Jesus went over and talked to Zacchaeus. He expressed his love in words. It's so very important, and yet so many people today fail miserably here. They don't know how to speak the words of love.

Have you seen the movie *Mr. & Mrs. Bridge*? It stars Paul Newman and Joanne Woodward. The film is about an American marriage during the late stages of middle age. The setting is in the 1930s and 1940s among the elite of Kansas City. Paul Newman plays a prominent straitlaced lawyer of crusty principle and extreme reserve, who has great difficulty expressing his love. So he tends to treat his obedient wife like a little child who should be either indulged or scolded.

In one poignant scene, Mr. and Mrs. Bridge are standing in the safe-deposit vault of a bank, when Mrs. Bridge suddenly asks her husband, "Do you love me?"

"If I didn't love you, I wouldn't be here," he retorts gruffly.

And then, softly, she says, "But couldn't you just tell me once in a while?"

She wants to hear it. She needs to hear it. She wants him to say it out loud. She needs warm reassurance. She wants to know that their love is alive and well. She needs to hear the words "I love you!" Don't we all? But look what happens to us. We forget to say the words, or neglect to say the words, or refuse to say the words. And that is so sad.

Husband and wife live together day in and day out; surely they love each other, but has it been said lately? Father and son, mother and daughter, sister and brother, all live together under the same roof. Surely they love one another, but how long has it been since it was said? Christian friends live near each other, serve in the same church, share the same pew, sing in the same choir, study in the same Sunday school class. Surely they love each other, but has it been said, has it been expressed, has it been verbalized?

Neighbors across a backyard fence, partners across an office desk—we assume our friends know how much we love them and value them and appreciate them—but still, louder than ever, the question rings out: Has it been said? Have we told them? Have we told them lately?

It's so simple, and yet so significant. Jesus walked over and said to Zacchaeus, "I love you. I care about you. You are important to me. I want to be your friend," and the impact of that was so potent that Zacchaeus was completely bowled over, turned upside down and inside out. He was converted from his head to his toes, from his heart to his hands. Talk about a conversion! His greed gave way to generosity. His selfishness gave way to service. His spirit of conceit gave way to the spirit of Christ.

That's what a spoken word of love can do for a person. It can absolutely change his or her life. So the point is clear: Get with the program. Give love a chance. Let it out. Splash it lavishly on everyone you meet. Become a conduit for God's love. Let the love of Christ flow through you and out to others. Speak the sounds of love. Express your love with words.

If you need to say "I love you" to someone, don't wait any longer, don't waste any more time. Say it loud and clear. Say it before the sun goes down tonight. Say it in the gracious spirit of Christ. Love can be expressed with words.

Love Can Be Expressed with Touch

Time after time in the Gospels, we see Jesus expressing his love and concern with a tender touch. Go back in time to the streets of Jericho. Can't you see Jesus giving Zacchaeus a helping hand as he climbs down from that sycamore tree? I can just picture that. Then as they walk away together toward Zacchaeus's house, can't you hear the angry crowd murmuring, "Look at that! Of all things, the Master's going home with Zacchaeus. Of all people! Does Jesus realize what he's doing? Doesn't he know what a sinner that greedy tax collector is?"

Just at that moment, when the complaints reach a fevered pitch, can't you see Jesus reaching over to compassionately pat Zacchaeus on the back, or put his hand gently on his shoulder, as if to say, "It's OK. I'm with you. I know all about you, Zacchaeus, and I still love you and care for you. And I'm still going to your house for dinner." All of that, expressed with a simple touch of love!

Way back then, Jesus knew something that psychiatrists have come to understand over the years—there is tremendous power in the touch of love. So much can be expressed with a hug or a handshake or a pat or a kiss. I feel so sorry for the person who, in early life, did not learn how to receive or give the touch of love.

Just this week, I ran across a beautiful story that makes the point. Some years ago, a little preschool girl was playing at home one day when she accidentally broke one of the family's most cherished heirlooms, an oriental vase that had been passed down from generation to generation. Because she knew its value, the little girl cried out when it broke. Hearing the crash and the cry, her mother came running. The child was in for a big surprise. She saw not anger on her mom's face, but relief.

"Oh, darling, I thought you were hurt," her mother said as she gathered the little girl into her loving arms, holding her tightly, rocking her gently, hugging her tenderly.

When that little girl grew up, she looked back on that event and said, "That was a great moment for me—

143

I discovered that day that *I* was the family treasure!" No question about it. Love can be expressed with words, and with touch.

Love Can Be Expressed with Actions

That day in Jericho long ago, Jesus went out on a limb for Zacchaeus. He knew he would be criticized for associating with this despised tax collector, but he also knew that Zacchaeus was a child of God who needed love and acceptance. So he made the sacrifice. For Zacchaeus's sake, for love's sake, he paid the price. There is nothing in this world more beautiful than that kind of love.

I remember a story about a college student who was attending a prestigious university in the east. The young freshman was visited one weekend by his father, who drove onto the university campus in his old dilapidated car.

When the father had left, some of the boy's classmates began to tease him, making fun of his father's old car. The young man replied, "Well, you can laugh if you want to, but let me tell you something. My dad could have had a new car. He had the money to buy it, but he wanted me to have an education at this school more than he wanted a new car for himself. The reason I'm here is because he chose to drive that old car. And I want you to know I love that old car—and I love the man driving it!"

There is nothing in this world more Christlike than an act of sacrificial love. Love can be expressed with words and with touch, but it is expressed most powerfully with actions. Jesus showed us how that day in Jericho. Later, he showed us on a cross. Without question, the greatest promise of God is found here. On page after page of the Bible, the promise is underscored and repeated: God is Love! God loves us! God wants us to take up this ministry of love!

Epilogue

Some Things We Can't Repay, But We Can Pass Them On

Have you ever been participating in a conversation with a group of people—words are being spoken, thoughts are being verbalized, beliefs are being shared, opinions are being articulated—when suddenly, out of the blue, someone expresses an idea that jumps out at you, captivates you, invigorates you, inspires you. It amplifies and reverberates in your brain—an idea that seems big and timeless and universally true, an idea that explodes into your mind as if it were capitalized and written in red, with several exclamation points to trumpet home its truth!

I had just such an experience recently. Sitting with close friends around a dinner table in the glow of candlelight after a sumptuous meal, the conversation turned somewhat philosophical and sentimental. We began talking about crisis moments in our lives and how, in those difficult moments, there were those special people who rose to the occasion, to "be there" for us, to help us in generous and compassionate ways.

One young woman told of being in an emergency situation some years before, when one of her children became seriously ill. She told of a neighbor who had sensed the seriousness of her dilemma and rushed to her side in that moment that was so traumatic for them, to help her and her family so graciously and sacrificially.

As she described that moment with her sick child and the neighbor who had come through for her in such a loving way, she was moved to tears and said, "There is just no way I could ever fully express my gratitude to that friend for all she did for us that night. There is simply no way I could ever repay her."

Then someone else in the group spoke up with that something that "lit up my mind": "You know, it's a fact of life that there are some things we can't repay, but we can pass them on!" That was it! That was the big idea that rattled in my head, and I thought to myself, "I wish I had said that, because that's such a big part of the gospel. Why didn't I think of that? It's so true and so biblical. Some things we simply cannot repay, but we can pass them on!"

Some time ago as I was walking across the courtyard of our church, I met a woman who was one of our charter members. When she asked me what I would be preaching about that Sunday, I told her the title: "Some Things We Can't Repay, But We Can Pass Them On."

Immediately, she announced, "I have a good sermon illustration for you about that," and she shared it with me:

Some years ago when we were in the Air Force, we were stationed in Germany. The first week we were there, my husband had a heart attack. He was only thirty-one years old at the time. It was traumatic.

We have only been there for a few days, so we didn't have a church yet to turn to. We had two babies in diapers, we didn't know anybody, and we were in a strange foreign country. I didn't know what to do. Suddenly, a neighbor who had heard of our problem appeared, and she said, "Go be with your husband! I'll take good care of your babies." She set me free to go to the hospital and make the decisions that needed to be made, and give my husband the TLC he so much needed.

Of course, in time my husband recovered fully, and after the crisis was over, I said to this good neighbor who had saved us in that difficult hour, "How can I ever repay you?" And she gave an answer I will never forget. She said, "The only way you can repay me is to do something like that for someone else sometime." And over the years, I have had several opportunities to do just that— to pass it on, to pass on to someone else her act of compassion.

Some things in life we can't repay. So what do we do? We try to pass them on to others. Think of all the things we could never repay.

The Love of Our Parents

We know the gracious, generous love our parents gave to us. We can't repay that. There's no way. All we can do is pass that love on to our children.

The Gift of a Church

The pioneers of the church dreamed it, and by the grace of God, they built it, and now they have given it to us. Next time you walk into your church, look around you at what you have there, and think of those remarkable people of faith who went before. God forbid that we should ever take the church for granted.

Sir Christopher Wren was the architect who built the magnificent St. Paul's Cathedral in London. When he died, he was buried inside the church, with this simple inscription: "Christopher Wren. If you seek his monument, look around you." That could be said of all those pioneers who started churches: "If you seek their monument, look around you." How do we repay them for what they did as the instruments of God? We can't repay that. All we can do is be the church and keep it strong, hold it high, carry it forward, and pass on that great heritage of faith to the next generation.

Some things we can't repay. All we can do is pass them on. I could go on and on, listing things we can't repay— a job opportunity, a word of recommendation, a touch of encouragement, a friendship during a crisis, a special lesson someone taught us, an act of love when we felt down and out, an expression of support when we were in desperate need, a comforting presence when our hearts were heavy.

And what about God and all we owe God! Grace, pardon, redemption, salvation, deliverance, healing, atonement, reconciliation, love—there's no way we can repay God for these gracious gifts. All we can do is accept them in faith, try to live in God's generous spirit, and be the instruments by which God's grace and love are passed on to others. Let me tell you about some of God's gifts that we can attempt to pass on.

The Promise of Acceptance

If Jesus walked into the sanctuary of your church next Sunday morning, where would he sit? You know what I think? I believe Jesus would look around a bit and find the person who is in the most need, and slip in beside that person. The one who is most lonely, the one feeling the most pain, the one who is hurting most right now— that's the one Jesus would choose to sit with. That's the one our Lord would reach out to, the one he would touch with the gift of gracious acceptance.

Some years ago, when K. C. Jones was coach of the Boston Celtics basketball team, he became famous for his unique ability to give his players some unforgettable words of encouragement when they needed it most. If a player scored fifty points or made the game-winning basket, he would not say much more than "nice game." But when a player was down and really struggling, Coach Jones would be there to comfort and help and inspire.

All-star forward Kevin McHale asked Coach Jones about this one day, and K. C. Jones answered: "Kevin, after you've made the winning basket, you've got 15,000 people cheering for you, TV commentators come rushing toward you, and everybody is giving you high fives. You don't need me then. When you need a friend most is when nobody is cheering."

Throughout the pages of the Bible, God repeats this sacred promise—to be there for us—to love us and support us, to strengthen us and accept us, to befriend us when nobody else is cheering. We can't repay God's acceptance of us, but we can pass that on to others. We can live in that gracious spirit.

The Promise of Forgiveness

When we receive forgiveness for wrongs we have done or things we have left undone, the best thing we can do is take on that spirit of mercy in our dealings and relationships with others and pass it on.

Jesus once told a parable about this, the parable of the unmerciful servant, in which a king forgives an enormous debt. A servant owes him some $10 million, and the king forgives the debt. Then the servant, who has just been forgiven this gigantic debt, goes out of the palace into the street. And there he sees a fellow servant who owes him $20. The forgiven servant runs over, grabs the other man by the throat, and demands his $20. When the fellow servant is unable to pay, the unmerciful servant (who has just been forgiven a debt of $10 million) has the man who can't pay him $20 dollars cast into prison.

When the king finds out about this, he is infuriated. He rebukes the unmerciful servant and sends him to prison. Now, the point of the parable is obvious: Since God (the King of kings) has forgiven us so much, then we ought to be forgiving like that, merciful like that, compassionate like that, toward others. This is what Zacchaeus did in Luke 19. Christ forgave him, and Zacchaeus came down from the sycamore tree, trying to set things right with others. Zacchaeus realized that God's gracious promise of forgiveness can't be repaid or earned. It can only be humbly accepted—and passed on to others.

The Promise of Kindness

My father died as a result of an automobile accident when I was thirteen years old. I'll never forget what happened the following night. As we stood by my father's casket at the funeral home, scores of people came by—all kinds of people from all walks of life.

Some of them I knew quite well; some I had never seen before. But they all came and spoke to us to express their sympathy. And almost every one of them said the same thing: "Jim, your dad was kind to me." Even though I was only thirteen at the time, I decided then and there that the best tribute I could pay to my dad was to take up his torch of kindness. From that moment, I have tried to be a kind person. I haven't always succeeded, but I have tried, and I am still trying to let my father's kindness live on in me.

Please hold that in your mind for a moment and remember with me what a kind person Jesus was! We give up on people, we write them off, we decide that they are beyond redemption. But Jesus never did that. He never relinquished his loving-kindness. He was kind all the way to the cross.

So the best tribute we can pay our Lord is to take up his torch of kindness—to love as he loved, to care as he cared, to live as he lived, to the very last, in the spirit of acceptance, forgiveness, and kindness.

Suggestions for Leading a Study of James W. Moore's

Standing on the Promises or Sitting on the Premises?

John D. Schroeder

This book by James W. Moore shows that when we stand on the promises of Scripture, we discover the richness and fullness that God intended for our lives. This study guide was created to help make this experience beneficial for both you and members of your group. Here are some thoughts on how you can help your group:

1. Distribute the book to participants before your first meeting and request that they come having read the first chapter. You may want to limit the size of your group to increase participation.

2. Begin your sessions on time. Your participants will appreciate your promptness. You may wish to begin your first session with introductions and a brief time to get acquainted. Start each session by reading aloud the snapshot summary of the chapter for the day.

3. Select discussion questions and activities in advance. Note that the first question is a general question designed to get discussion going. The last question is designed to summarize the discussion. Feel free to change the order of the listed questions and to create your own questions. Allow a set amount of time for the questions and activities.

4. Remind participants that all questions are valid as part of the learning process. Encourage their participation in discussion by saying there are no "wrong" answers and that all input will be appreciated. Invite participants to share their thoughts, personal stories, and ideas as their comfort level allows.

5. Some questions may be more difficult to answer than others. If you ask a question and no one responds, begin the discussion by venturing an answer yourself. Then ask for comments and other answers. Remember that some questions may have multiple answers.

6. Ask the question *Why?* or *Why do you believe that?* to help continue a discussion and give it greater depth.

7. Give everyone a chance to talk. Keep the conversation moving. Occasionally you may want to direct a question to a specific person who has been quiet. *Do you have anything to add?* is a good follow-up question to ask another person. If the topic of conversation gets off track, move ahead by asking the next question in your study guide.

8. Before moving from questions to activities, ask group members if they have any questions that have not been answered. Remember that as a leader, you do not have to know all the answers. Some answers may come from group members. Other answers may even need a bit of research. Your job is to keep the discussion moving and to encourage participation.

9. Review the activity in advance. Feel free to modify it or to create your own activity. Encourage participants to try the "At home" activity.

10. Following the conclusion of the activity, close with a brief prayer, praying either the printed prayer from the study guide or a prayer of your own. If your group desires, pause for individual prayer petitions.

11. Be grateful and supportive. Thank group members for their ideas and participation.

12. You are not expected to be a perfect leader. Just do the best you can by focusing on the participants and the lesson. God will help you lead this group.

13. Enjoy your time together!

Suggestions for Participants

1. What you will receive from this study will be in direct proportion to your involvement. Be an active participant!

2. Please make a point to attend all sessions and to arrive on time so that you can receive the greatest benefit.
3. Read the chapter and review the study guide questions prior to the meeting. You may want to jot down questions you have from the reading and also answers to some of the study guide questions.
4. Be supportive and appreciative of your group leader as well as the other members of your group. You are on a journey together.
5. Your participation is encouraged. Feel free to share your thoughts about the material being discussed.
6. Pray for your group and your leader.

Introduction

Are You Standing on the Promises or Sitting on the Premises?

Snapshot Summary

This chapter asks whether we embrace the promises of God or whether we simply trudge through life with no mission and no purpose, and it explores how the Holy Spirit gives us comfort, courage, and a commission.

Reflection / Discussion Questions

1. What issues and questions are raised by the title of this book? What do you hope to gain from this study?
2. Reflect on / discuss the importance and the characteristics of promises. What goes into a promise?
3. Recall a promise made to you that was kept. Why is that promise memorable?
4. What promise does Jesus make in John 14:15-17?
5. Reflect on / discuss different ways in which God comforts us.
6. Why does it often feel as though God is closer to us when we are in pain?

7. Give your own definition of *courage* and give an example of what it means to be courageous.

8. Reflect on / discuss different types of commissions or special jobs God gives us.

9. How are we to respond to God's promises?

10. What are some examples of comfort, courage, and commission that are found in the Bible?

Activities

As a group: Write down promises you will keep this week that relate to comfort, courage, or commission. Carry your promise or promises with you. Share them with the group, if you desire.

At home: Meditate this week on the importance of promises, those God has made to us, and those you have made to God and to others.

Prayer: *Dear God, thank you for the many promises you have made to us. Help us to remember them and to rely on your faithfulness. Help us be faithful in our promises to you and to others. Amen.*

Chapter 1

The Promise of God's Love: The Greatest Gift

Snapshot Summary

This chapter reminds us of the width, the depth, and the power of God's love.

Reflection / Discussion Questions

1. Discuss the importance of love and what it means to you. When and why is love often promised to others?

2. List some fears people have concerning love. What's the greatest fear?

3. Discuss why love is such a powerful force. Why is love more powerful than hate?

4. Reflect on / discuss ways in which Jesus acted out the message of John 3:16 during Holy Week.

5. Name some words or phrases that describe how it feels to be loved.

6. How should we respond to the promise of God's love?

7. Discuss what it means that God's love is worldwide yet very personal.

8. Share a time when you felt or relied upon the promise of God's love.

9. How has God's sacrificial love touched your life? How has it changed you?

10. Describe some ways we can share God's love with others.

Activities

As a group: Create John 3:16 bookmarks for your Bible using markers, pens, paper, and crayons. Include the words of John 3:16, along with an illustration of its message. Share your bookmark with the rest of the group.

At home: Give the gift of love to others this week. Show your love through words and deeds.

Prayer: *Dear God, thank you for your unconditional love. Help us to love others unconditionally and to remember the words and the spirit of John 3:16. Amen.*

Chapter 2

The Promise of God's Presence with Us: Where the Risen Christ Meets Us

Snapshot Summary

This chapter shows how God is always there, offering encouragement, forgiveness, and direction.

Reflection / Discussion Questions

1. Share how the promise of God's presence makes you feel.

2. Reread John 21:15-19. What can we learn from this Scripture?

3. In what ways are we often like Simon Peter?

4. Share a time when you needed encouragement and received it.

5. Why did Peter need encouragement, and how was it provided?

6. Describe how it feels to be forgiven. What are some of the blessings of forgiveness?

7. How is a person changed through forgiveness? Give an example.

8. Name some of the ways God provides direction for our lives.

9. Share a time when you felt a sense of God giving you direction.

10. How have your reading, reflection, and discussion of this chapter given you new insight or challenged you?

Activities

As a group: Discuss: What reminds you that God is always present? Using available resources, create small reminders that you can carry with you to let you know that God is always with you.

At home: Increase your awareness of God's presence in your life. Meditate on opening your eyes, heart, and mind to the fullness of God and to God's ways.

Prayer: *Dear God, thank you for walking with me in good times and in times of trouble. Direct my path, Lord. Forgive me when I falter. Remind me of your constant presence, along with your constant encouragement and love. Amen.*

Chapter 3

The Promise of a Rock-Solid Foundation: Building on the Rock

Snapshot Summary

This chapter explores the rock-solid commitment, trust, and love of God.

Reflection / Discussion Questions

1. Reflect on / discuss the wisdom and warnings contained in Matthew 7:21, 24-27.

2. What are some of the reasons a person's faith may be weak and lacking in any real influence on his or her life?

3. What does the phrase "storms of life" mean to you? What effect can the storms of life have on a weak faith?

4. What does it mean to act on the words of Jesus? What does that look like in your life?

5. What is needed in order to build a stable house of faith?

6. Reflect on / discuss the traits and attitude of a person who possesses a rock-solid commitment to Christ.

7. What are some ways in which a person can grow stronger in faith and commitment?

8. Explain in your own words what it means to have complete trust in the Lord.

9. How does a person attain a rock-solid love of God and others?

10. What are some of the costs and challenges involved in building a rock-solid foundation? What are the benefits?

Activities

As a group: Draw a large wall made up of stones to depict a rock-solid foundation. Work as a group to label each of the stones with a trait or a quality that contributes to a strong foundation.

Study Guide

At home: Meditate upon the foundation of your faith. How solid is it? Check for cracks and shifting sand. What can you do to build a strong foundation of faith?

Prayer: Dear God, thank you for your promise of a rock-solid commitment to us in all areas of our lives. Help us build our lives on the truth of your word found in the Bible. Amen.

Chapter 4

The Promise of Peace: Give Peace a Chance

Snapshot Summary

This chapter provides three ways we can become peacemakers in the world.

Reflection / Discussion Questions

1. When you hear the word *peace*, what images come to mind?

2. Reflect on / discuss the biggest threats to peace in the world and in your community.

3. What are some actions people can take to bring about peace and to reduce violence?

4. The author says that our streets, schools, and courtrooms, apart from real war, have become modern-day battle zones of sorts. Do you agree? Why or why not?

5. Why is peacemaking a sign of spiritual maturity?

6. Why is it important for us to make peace with ourselves? How can we achieve inner peace?

7. When you are not at peace with yourself, how does it feel, and how does it affect your life?

8. What are some of the barriers that prevent us from making peace with others?

9. Reflect on / discuss what it means to be at peace with God. How do you achieve this peace?

10. What are some words and phrases that peacemakers might use?

Activities

As a group: Using art supplies, make a peace bumper sticker that uses words, pictures, or other symbols. Share your finished creation with the rest of the group and talk about its meaning.

At home: Pray, asking God to make you a peacemaker. Look for opportunities to be a peacemaker at home or at work and try where possible to prevent problems before they arise.

Prayer: *Dear God, thank you for the promise of peace and for offering each of us the role of peacemaker. Help us learn and live by the words and actions of peacemakers. Amen.*

Chapter 5

The Promise of Victory: From Victims to Victors

Snapshot Summary

This chapter shows how God helps us rise above our circumstances, our defeats, and our despair.

Reflection / Discussion Questions

1. Share a time when you experienced a victory. How did it feel? If you had not achieved this victory, how would you have felt?

2. Reread 2 Corinthians 4:8-14. In your own words, what is this passage telling us?

3. In general terms, describe the "culture of victimhood" mind-set.

4. To any degree that a person can control, does attitude play a role in distinguishing between being a victim and being a victor? Explain.

5. Name some ways you can let God help you rise above your circumstances.

6. What steps can we take to recover from a defeat?

7. Share a time when God helped you cope with defeat or despair.

8. In what ways can you minister to others who are suffering from defeat or despair?

9. What do we need to do to receive the promises of God?

10. What additional insights or questions from this chapter would you like to explore?

Activities

As a group: Create a list of keys to a victorious Christian life. Include actions, attitudes, phrases, examples from the Bible, and examples from your own life experiences.

At home: Reflect upon upcoming challenges in life. What do you need to come out a winner? What help do you need from God?

Prayer: *Dear God, thank you for giving us the ability to rise above circumstances, defeat, and despair. Help us to remember that because of you, we will never walk alone. Amen.*

Chapter 6

The Promise of Conversion: Turning Inkblots into Angels

Snapshot Summary

This chapter highlights how God can take bad things and turn them into good things.

Reflection / Discussion Questions

1. Share a time in your life when God turned an inkblot into an angel.

2. Reread Romans 8:28, 31, 35, 37-39 and summarize the meaning of this passage in your own words.

3. Why do we sometimes struggle with our problems instead of giving them to God?

4. Reflect on / discuss some of the hardships experienced by the apostle Paul and how he coped with difficulties. How did God turn Paul's inkblots into angels?

5. Give an example of how despair can be turned into hope. What is needed for this to occur?

6. What signs of hope do you see in our world today?

7. How do you turn a problem into an opportunity? What roles do *attitude* and *creativity* play in this?

8. What is the role of prayer when it comes to turning bad situations around?

9. Share a time when a personal defeat eventually became a victory. What made the difference?

10. What additional insights or questions from this chapter would you like to explore?

Activities

As a group: Using the appropriate art supplies, create your own simple inkblots on a piece of paper. After each group member has created an inkblot, exchange inkblots with one another and let group members create angels from the inkblots they have been given.

At home: Reflect upon the victories and defeats you have experienced in life. What did you learn from your victories? from your defeats? How will you let God guide you in meeting future challenges?

Prayer: *Dear God, thank you for giving us the promise of hope and for reminding us that ultimate victory rests in you. Help us to see and take advantage of opportunities to lift others out of despair and to be your messengers and servants of hope in the world. Amen.*

Chapter 7

The Promise of the Holy Spirit: Say Yes to Life

Snapshot Summary

This chapter shows how the Holy Spirit empowers us as Christians to face the future with hope.

Reflection / Discussion Questions

1. What issues were the disciples dealing with after the crucifixion of Jesus?

2. What instructions did Jesus give to his disciples after Jesus' resurrection?

3. How did the Holy Spirit change the lives of the disciples?

4. According to the author, what is the promise of Pentecost?

5. How does a person receive the Holy Spirit? What are some signs that the Holy Spirit dwells within you?

6. Explain what it means that the Holy Spirit allows us to say yes to life.

7. What causes some people to "mummify"? What do they miss out on when this occurs?

8. Give an example of what it means to say yes to other people. Can you do so without saying a word? Explain.

9. Share a time when you struggled until you said yes to God. How were you changed in the process?

10. What power does the Holy Spirit provide? How does it make a difference in the daily life of a Christian?

Activities

As a group: Use a hymnal or the Bible to locate words and phrases that describe the Holy Spirit and how it changes us.

At home: Look for opportunities to say yes to life this week.

Prayer: *Dear God, thank you for the promise of the Holy Spirit. Thank you for all that the Holy Spirit empowers us to do in your name. May we be faithful disciples and strive always to do your will. Amen.*

Chapter 8

The Promise of Hope: The Light Shines, and the Darkness Cannot Overcome It

Snapshot Summary

This chapter shows us how the light of God overcomes the darkness of ignorance, prejudice, and sin.

Reflection / Discussion Questions

1. Share a time when you experienced light from God during a dark moment in your life.

2. Reflect on / discuss types of darkness in our world today.

3. How have you been affected by crime and violence? What frightens or concerns you the most?

4. Why do Christians have good reason to be optimistic in troubled times?

5. Give some examples of the darkness of ignorance in our world today.

6. Why are the Ten Commandments timeless? How do they help us?

7. Share a time when you felt or witnessed the darkness of prejudice.

8. What are some ways we can share the promise of hope with others?

9. How do you escape from the darkness of sin? What words or actions provide escape and hope?

10. In your own words, explain the promise and power of hope. Describe what it means to you.

Activities

As a group: Go on a hunt for hope. Use newspapers, magazines, the Bible, hymnals, and other resources to locate messages, symbols, and promises of hope. Compile a group list.

At home: On a piece of paper, make a list of your hopes and dreams. Reflect on the role God plays in providing hope in your life.

Prayer: *Dear God, thank you for providing beacons of hope that overcome the darkness of ignorance, prejudice, and sin. Show us how to shine the light of your love upon those who need it in our world. Amen.*

Chapter 9

The Promise of Resurrection: When Easter Calls Your Name

Snapshot Summary

This chapter highlights the joy, encouragement, and forgiveness that God provides through the Resurrection.

Reflection / Discussion Questions

1. Why do you think so many people believe in life after death?

2. What are your thoughts on Mary Magdalene's Easter-morning experience?

3. In what way was Mary herself resurrected on Easter morning?

4. Explain what it means to personally experience the risen Lord.

5. What are some of the reasons people fail to accept or follow Jesus?

6. How does the promise of resurrection empower your life and your faith?

7. The risen Lord is still speaking. What is Jesus saying to us today?

8. Reflect on / discuss the joy of Easter and ways in which that joy is expressed.

9. How can we share with others the encouragement to be found in Jesus' resurrection?

10. In what way does the resurrection of Jesus assure us of forgiveness?

Activities

As a group: Search the Bible to find examples of God's promise of resurrection and new life.

At home: Read accounts of the resurrection of Jesus as found in the Bible. Reflect on the meaning of Jesus' resurrection for your life.

Prayer: *Dear God, thank you for all the promises you have given in the resurrection of Jesus. Help us live each day with a grateful heart and in the spirit of new life. Amen.*

Chapter 10

The Promise of Happiness: The Roads to Happiness

Snapshot Summary

This chapter examines the different roads to happiness, including the roads to conversion, kindness, faith, and sacrificial love.

Reflection / Discussion Questions

1. Share something that brought you a moment of happiness.

2. What truths about happiness have you learned as you have grown older?

3. What are some things people often confuse with true happiness?

4. Reflect on / discuss reasons why there are so many unhappy people in the world.

5. In your own words, explain why Christ himself is the road to happiness.

6. What's the connection between happiness and forgiveness? between happiness and conversion?

7. Share a time when you were the recipient of someone's kindness. How did it make you feel?

8. What does it mean to have an unflinching confidence when it comes to faith? How easy or how difficult would that be for you? Explain your answer.

9. What are some of the ways we can live in the spirit of sacrificial love?

10. In times of unhappiness, what should we remember?

Activities

As a group: Draw a winding road that leads to happiness. Place signs and stops along the way.

At home: Bring unexpected happiness to another person this week. Be guilty of committing a kindness.

Prayer: *Dear God, thank you for paving the road to happiness through your Son, Jesus Christ. Help us follow the teaching of Jesus as we travel through life. Amen.*

Chapter 11

The Promise of Christlike Living: Do the Teachings of Jesus Still Work?

Snapshot Summary

This chapter looks at what it means to "turn the other cheek" and to live in the spirit of unconditional love.

Reflection / Discussion Questions

1. Do you personally find some of Jesus' sayings to be difficult to follow or understand? Explain your answer and, if possible, give an example.

2. How is the power of love the basis for the difficult sayings of Jesus?

3. What does "unconditional love" mean to you?

4. Are the sayings of Jesus practical or not practical in today's world? Explain.

5. Share a time when you faced a choice between retaliation and turning the other cheek.

6. What results follow from retaliation?

7. In what way does turning the other cheek mean strength rather than meekness or weakness?

8. What are some of the dangers of resentment?

9. What costs are there in following the teachings of Jesus?

10. In your own words, what does "Christlike living" involve?

Activities

As a group: Apply the teachings of Jesus in this lesson to your behavior as a victim of a robbery or a car accident; how should a Christian respond in that situation? Select similar situations and talk about what a Christian should do and should not do.

At home: Look inside yourself and find a situation that is troubling you. Ponder how you can apply the teachings of Jesus and "turn the other cheek."

Prayer: *Dear God, thank you for challenging us to live as Jesus did. Grant us the strength to respond in love to the difficulties we face in life. Amen.*

Chapter 12

The Promise of the Bible: Superstars, Smug Spectators, and Sacrificial Servants

Snapshot Summary

This chapter tells us that the Bible clearly teaches us that we are called to be servants.

Reflection / Discussion Questions

1. Reflect on / discuss the benefits of reading the Bible on a regular basis.

2. What are some of the ways in which the Bible equips a person for life?

3. How does the Bible help you determine what is true, right, valuable, and good? Give some examples of how the Bible instructs us.

4. Share which is your favorite book of the Bible and tell why it is your favorite.

5. What are the benefits of memorizing key verses of the Bible?

6. What does the Bible say about being a servant to others?

7. Name some of the great servants in the Bible or accounts of selfless acts of service to others.

8. How did Jesus model the role of servant for us?

9. Share a time when someone showed you what it means to be a sacrificial servant.

10. List some ideas on how to live in the spirit of sacrificial service.

Activities

As a group: Create a "Biblical Measuring Stick" containing truths and topics located within the Bible. Draw the measuring stick on paper or on a board and let everyone in the group contribute truths and topics.

At home: Write down a number of ways you can be a sacrificial servant this week and put as many of your ideas into practice as possible.

Prayer: *Dear God, thank you for the promises, wisdom, and encouragement contained within the Bible. Help us follow the teachings of the Bible to become the sacrificial servants our communities need. Amen.*

Chapter 13

The Promise of New Life: Launch Out into the Deep

Snapshot Summary

This chapter encourages us to launch out into the depths of gratitude, penitence, and commitment.

Reflection / Discussion Questions

1. When you hear the words "new life," what comes to mind and why?
2. Reread Luke 5:1-11. What life lessons do we learn from this passage and how do they apply to us today?
3. Give examples of some of the times in life when people need to launch out into the deep and find new life.
4. Share a time when you needed and discovered new life. As you are comfortable doing so, talk about your journey.
5. Give some reasons why some people remain in the "shallows" instead of enjoying the depths of life and faith.
6. How does it feel to be the recipient of an act of generosity? Give an example from your own experience.
7. Why is our expression of penitence so often half-hearted and shallow?
8. What are some indications or characteristics of genuine repentance?

9. Why are people often frightened of commitment?
10. Describe some ways a person can begin a new lease on life.

Activities

As a group: Have your own thanksgiving celebration, regardless of the time of year. On the "menu," include a list of God's blessings. Discuss ways to be generous to others. Draw a large turkey and fill it with truths that take away human hunger.

At home: Take a step out of your comfort zone and into the depths of new life this week.

Prayer: *Dear God, thank you for your promise of new life that is available to us at all times. Help us to live life with a sense of purpose, excitement, and wonder and help us contribute to improving the lives of those around us. Amen.*

Chapter 14

The Promise of Prayer: How Do We Pray and Why?

Snapshot Summary

This chapter reminds us to pray in the spirit of gratitude, forgiveness, and trust.

Reflection / Discussion Questions

1. Why do Christians pray? Why do *you* pray, and what do you pray *for*?
2. When you pray, what do you expect from God?
3. Share a time when you experienced the power of prayer.
4. What makes the Lord's Prayer so special and unique?
5. Do you agree with the author's characterization of prayer as friendship with God? Why or why not?

6. Reflect on / discuss what it means to pray in the spirit of gratitude.
7. What role does forgiveness play in prayer?
8. How is trust an important element of prayer?
9. Reflect on / discuss different ways in which prayer may be answered.
10. What additional insights or questions from this chapter would you like to explore?

Activities

As a group: Treat the Lord's Prayer as a treasure. On a small piece of paper, draw a treasure chest and, inside it, write out the Lord's Prayer (see Luke 11:1-4) to carry with you. Share with the group what having a personal relationship with Jesus Christ means to you.

At home: Reflect on *how* you pray and *why* you pray. Evaluate your prayer life. How might you improve your communication with God?

Prayer: *Dear God, thank you for the promise of prayer and for giving us the Lord's Prayer. Help us to pray in the spirit of gratitude, forgiveness, and trust, knowing that you are always listening to us. Amen.*

Chapter 15

The Promise of Compassion: Ways to Express Love

Snapshot Summary

This chapter shows us how love can be expressed through words, through touch, and through actions.

Reflection / Discussion Questions

1. Give one example of how love has changed your life.
2. What lessons for our lives today are found in the encounter of Jesus and Zacchaeus?

3. Reflect on / discuss some of the reasons people may find it difficult to express love.

4. How do people learn to love? What experiences shape our outlook?

5. Name some things that many people do not know about love.

6. What are some of the ways in which we receive love from God?

7. Why do people often fail to speak words of love to one another?

8. What does it mean to experience love in a touch? If possible, give an example.

9. Give an example of an act of sacrificial love. What makes love in action so powerful?

10. Reflect on / discuss ways to become a conduit for God's love.

Activities

As a group: Locate favorite acts of love found in the Bible. Give all group members the opportunity to contribute a favorite example and share why that particular biblical example of an act of love stands out for them.

At home: Reflect on God's love for you and how you have responded.

Prayer: *Dear God, thank you for the promise of compassion. Help us not to hold love inside of us but to let it out and express it to others. Amen.*

Epilogue

Some Things We Can't Repay, But We Can Pass Them On

Snapshot Summary

This chapter looks at some of the many blessings and gifts that come from God and from others. We cannot repay these blessings, but we can pass them on.

Reflection / Discussion Questions

1. Share something you received that you can never repay.
2. How does it feel to be on the receiving end of great compassion?
3. Reflect on / discuss different creative ways to pass along love to others.
4. Using your own words, explain God's promise of acceptance.
5. Give some reasons why we should pass forgiveness on to others.
6. Share a kindness that was passed along to you during your childhood.
7. Why are money and gifts commonly used to try to repay debts? Why do they fall short?
8. Name a crisis that can leave behind a huge debt. Name some ways people help others in times of crisis.
9. What debts do we owe God? How can we respond to God's gifts to us?
10. How have your reading, reflection, and discussion of this book personally enriched you? What additional questions or insights would you like to explore?

Activities

As a group: Hold an informal graduation party to celebrate your completion of this book and this study, with *Promises* as your theme.

At home: Reflect on your experience of this book. Think and pray about any changes you would like to make in your life as a result of your participation.

Prayer: *Dear God, thank you for all of your promises to us. Help us claim them and know that we can rely on them, that we may discover all of the blessings and the fullness you intend for our lives. Amen.*